EACE BEE, HONEY BEE,
AND PRISCILLA BEE

CHRONIC
MENTAL ILLNESS:
A LIVING NIGHTMARE

authorHOUSE®

AuthorHouse™
1663 Liberty Drive
Bloomington, IN 47403
www.authorhouse.com
Phone: 1 (800) 839-8640

Published by AuthorHouse 07/16/2015

ISBN: 978-1-4969-6771-8 (sc)
ISBN: 978-1-4969-6770-1 (e)

Library of Congress Control Number: 2015901582

Print information available on the last page.

Any people depicted in stock imagery provided by Thinkstock are models, and such images are being used for illustrative purposes only. Certain stock imagery © Thinkstock.

This book is printed on acid-free paper.

Because of the dynamic nature of the Internet, any web addresses or links contained in this book may have changed since publication and may no longer be valid. The views expressed in this work are solely those of the author and do not necessarily reflect the views of the publisher, and the publisher hereby disclaims any responsibility for them.

Dr. Patricia L. Pickles, the editor, is not a medical doctor. She has a Ph.D. in education and administration. The book is intended to share information only and should not be interpreted as providing medical advice.

Pseudo names have been provided in order to protect the identity and privacy of individuals.

Dedication

Compassion is the ability to put yourself in the place of another, without judgement, criticism, or the need to control. It is realizing what someone else is going through. It is sharing your experiences in the hope of helping someone else in a similiar situation. This book is dedicated to: families, individuals experiencing mental confusion, and caregivers. I am not a medical doctor but I do have first hand experience. Usually, when one family member is affected, it impacts other family members as well.

By sharing our family story with integrity and dignity, we want you to know that you are not alone. The struggles and cries for compassion, deserve to be heard. We want to inspire others with hope and faith. Combined efforts make a difference. United together, altering attitudes and demanding justice for those with thought disorders becomes easier. Significant change takes the will of a village, action from the people, and the heart of our nation. This is our American dream.

"One of the great conundrums with America health care is the great disparity between the need for mental health care and the lack of resources to address the huge need. Of course this is nothing new. Over the course of our history the mentally ill have been ignored, abused, victimized, imprisoned, misdiagnosed and just generally kicked to the curb. Dr. Pickles' book is a welcome addition to the growing demand for compassion, science, equality and justice for those suffering with mental illness."

Danny K. Davis
U.S. Representative, Illinois

Acknowledgments

In a world full of fear and lack of knowledge regarding mental illness, it takes a great deal of courage for the Bee family to share their personal story and talk about a topic that is still taboo. Priscilla is the mother of a son with schizophrenia. The book is written from the mother's perspective but there are contributions from, her son Eace Bee and, her daughter, Honey Bee. Illness is a family affair. Sharing their knowledge and experience so that others can benefit is their greatest gift in the world, and in their hearts they truly believe that there is a family somewhere who can use what they now know. Stop blaming yourself for what you didn't know. We learn from one another, from researching, and from experiencing.

Priscilla also acknowledges Samuel Bryant for sharing his vision for this book more than a decade ago. Thanks to Adrienne Kennedy and Quevarra Moten for their contributions that go beyond this book. Appreciation is also extended to, the Honorable Avel Louise Gordly, the Honorable Royce West, The Honorable Danny Davis, and Mary Gilbertie from Nami national.

Contents

Dedication v

Acknowledgments vii

About the Book xiii

Introduction: It's Not Stigma, It's Indifference xv

Preface: Coming Out of the Mental Illness "Closet" xvii

Why We Wrote The Book And Ended The Silence 1

    Consumer's Voice – My Experiences Are Valuable 2

    Mother's Voice – My Son's Story Deserves To Be Told With Dignity 2

    Our Story 3

    Support 3

    Education 3

    Advocacy 4

    Resiliency 4

Early Detection and Intervention 7

    Historical Backdrop 8

    Not Recognizing or Understanding What We Observe 9

    Medication for Young Children 9

    Building Relationships 10

    Special Education 10

    Public Schools' IEP: 11

    Identify the Need 11

    Examine Human Resources 11

    Provide Special Services and Opportunities 12

Emotional Stages, Conclusions and Suggestions 13

    Victim's Story 14

    Denial 14

    Frustration 14

    My Reality 14

    Hopelessness 15

    Reluctant Acceptance 15

    Recovery 15

NAMI must capture broad awareness and brand recognition on par with the American Cancer Society, the American Heart Association, and the American Diabetes Association. It's NAMI's time to claim its own spotlight as the leader in addressing the last (often forgotten and invisible) of these **Big Four** health issues. We must stand together, side by side, to promote research, prevention, education, treatment, and wellness for all our citizens. Our culture will be judged not merely by its will and capacity to address the obvious health and wellness issues, but by its humanity and civility in addressing mental illnesses and the toll these illnesses take in our lives, our families, our workplaces, and our communities.

Adrienne Kennedy, board of directors, NAMI
National trainer for NAMI Basics
State trainer for NAMI Signature Programs: Family-to-Family, Family Support Group, Parents and Teachers as Allies
(Honored as the recipient of NAMI's 2013 Education Leadership Award)

Under Adrienne's leadership as affiliate president (2011-2013), NAMI Austin was honored with NAMI's 2013 Affiliate of the Year Award.

Preface:

Coming Out of the Mental Illness "Closet"

Over the last thirteen years, I've held a silence that at times made me feel dead inside. My brother, I, and close family and friends know our journey and everything that has come with it. Our mother has battled mental illness for years.

In observance of "going green" for the National Alliance on Mental Illness in May, and Minority Awareness Month in July 2014, I wanted to share a snippet of my story. Over the last ten weeks I have been teaching a class called Family-to-Family, sponsored by NAMI Austin. It teaches family members of those with mental illness how to take care of their loved ones and how to take care of themselves. In one of the classes we talked about coming out of the closet about mental illness. I told the class this: "Sometimes the heaviest load you carry could be the very thing to lift the load off someone else." I paused for a moment because in that very second I knew I needed to share my story about my mom.

Living with someone with paranoid schizophrenia changed my outlook on life and on what is really important. I pondered the questions and remarks I received from friends and family. *Girl how your mamma doing? I called your mamma and she seems different. I have called your mom over and over again and she is not answering, what's up? Girl, it is just stress, it will pass.* I would pause awkwardly because at that moment, as her advocate and caregiver, I had to decide whether the speaker could handle the truth, and whether he or she might use it to hurt her, or go and gossip about her to others. Until one day God said to me, "You are not equipped to protect her like I can."

We had to process and grieve over who our mother was and embrace the amazing woman she is today! Did you know that one in every four adults battles mental illness? Did you know that one in every five children battles mental illness? Depression, anxiety, bipolar disorder, schizophrenia, and eating disorders, just to name a few. One day God smiled on my family and introduced me to the National Alliance on Mental Illness (NAMI). It gave me resources to help us navigate getting Mom help. That amazing day in 2009 changed our lives for the better. I pray that this little piece of our story encourages someone to fight the stigma of mental illness. *Mentally ill* does not mean *crazy*— what is crazy is this society. Our culture has conditioned us to be reluctant to even talk about it! For help and resources in your area contact NAMI. You can learn more about NAMI at www.nami.org.

Quevarra Moten, May 2014
Founder of Quevarra Speaks
Director of Student Success & Persistence,
Central Texas College, Killeen

WHY WE WROTE THE BOOK
AND ENDED THE SILENCE

2014 Adult Mental Health Awareness Statewide Poetry Contest
5th Place Winner,

Eace Bee

I actually heard the preacher, crystal clear, for the first time when I went to church. He said, "Come out of the wilderness and into the kindness. If you don't take this opportunity you can be led into devastation; let yourself be shown." I was with my sister and her friend and I caught the Holy Ghost. I floated over to my sister's friend and laid my head on her breast to finish listening to the preacher. I am certain the preacher must have seen me. As he continued to talk, I felt like he was talking directly to me. He said spirits are disguised as sicknesses. I felt emotionally sick. Then I heard a voice tell me that I needed "special milk" from the girl where my head softly lay.

But if any provide not for his own, and especially for those of his own house, he has denied the faith, and is worse than an infidel.

1 Timothy 5:8, King James Version

Why We Wrote the Book and Ended the Silence

This book was written to reach out to other families who face unimaginable pain and hardship due to mental anguish. By telling our story, we hope to provide a voice for others in similar situations. We also want to promote healing, support and education. Our ultimate goal is to ignite the hunger for resiliency and recovery.

Consumer's Voice – My Experiences Are Valuable

My name is Eace Bee. I felt compelled to write this book with my mom and my sister because like those in the movies *Rain Man, A Beautiful Mind, Frankie and Alice, Call Me Crazy, As Good as It Gets, For Colored Girls,* and *Hope,* I have something of value to share with others. My experiences, for the most part, have shown me that society remains ignorant and stigmatizes brain and emotional disorders. I live in a cold, cold world. I can only go through so much. I have learned to find relief through books, writing, and drawing. Through books I can go where I want to go and be who I want to be. I learned that books and writing make me happy. I am taking this opportunity to lend my voice to others living in despair.

Mother's Voice – My Son's Story Deserves To Be Told With Dignity

My name is Priscilla Bee and my son is my hero. When I think about what he has had to endure, I know a lesser man could not have done it. Eace's story of hope needs to be told and it deserves to be told with integrity. My son is still inside his body. He is talented and creative and this book provides an opportunity to showcase his creative writing and artistic talent. Throughout the book, Eace's thoughts emerge where he can be seen as a valuable human being with real feelings. I am standing up for my son and in the process I have become an advocate for others like him. Letting go of the life that he once knew, so that he may live for today, is one hell of a transformation to have to go through.

Like most parents, I have always been afraid of passing away and leaving my children behind. But I have learned that the best and most valuable gift you can leave is something for others to prosper from and a truth that others can stand on. This contribution is important to my family but it is also important to other families struck by the debilitating and horrific experience of mental illness. This book was written through pain, compassion, and *agape* love.

Our Story

We want to tell our own story. Though others may speculate and attempt to tell our story, it is not theirs to tell. Others only have a superficial view and they have no idea what we really experience or go through. We understand that mental illness is a very scary and difficult subject to talk about and we fear what we don't understand. It took us many years to talk about the subject because we did not want to be stigmatized or labeled. We have learned that the worst prison one can live in is fear of what other people think. Wherever you are in your journey right now, we want to support you and encourage you in any way we can. When you tell your own story, you take power away from those who are gossiping behind your back anyway. Don't let stigma rob you of your voice.

We are turning our passion and lived experiences into a voice for others. In order to be a strong voice for mental illness we, the caregivers and families, must first accept ourselves. We can play a huge role in seeing the stigma of mental illness eradicated. Providing help, hope, and resiliency for ourselves and others is our intent.

This book is about the heart. We want to reach out to other families and communities to let them know: you are not alone in your struggle as providers and caregivers. Discrimination among the mentally ill is so widespread in this country that it is invisible because it is the norm. One of the worst things we can do to ourselves and our loved ones is remain isolated and voiceless. In the black community, we feel strongly about keeping our personal business private. Nevertheless, through our voices, we can make a difference in our own lives and in our own communities. We believe, together, our stories can unite us with one voice. By talking about the deep dark place of mental illness and bringing it into the light, we are healing ourselves

There is healing in writing. Reflecting and expressing your most powerful feelings and emotions on paper can change you on a deeper level. Although we began to keep a journal and write for ourselves, we now write to reach out and help others. We hope that others are empowered by our stories and gain a deeper understanding of the emotions, issues, and challenges we face.

Support

Provide appropriate support for your loved one. I will continue to search for every method available to make Eace feel valued and loved. He loves to write and draw. Writing helps people to express, explore, and explain the world they live in so that it becomes a safe, and more stable place for them. Writing is a way to process information and to be creative. For some, this activity is a way of processing complex experiences that bring about emotional piece.

Education

My family has actually experienced the trauma and unpredictability involved in caring for someone suffering from a thought disorder. To better assist my son, I had to learn more. I learned through trial and error and by researching, reading, asking questions, listening, and implementing proven tactics and strategies. In an attempt to raise awareness for others, I share what I learned and what still needs to be learned and discovered.

I took advantage of best-practice training opportunities sponsored through the National Alliance on Mental Illness (NAMI). I learned about NAMI opportunities through a "Sharing Hope" presentation at my church. While I continue to search for stability and a better life for Eace, the NAMI flagship signature programs, like *Family-to-Family* and *Parents and Teachers as Allies*, taught me how to separate symptoms of my son's illness from the person I know him to be. NAMI's *Family-to-Family* program was developed by Dr. Joyce Burland. I went from being a student in the program to teaching it. The NAMI program was declared an evidence-based practice in 2013. Every time I teach, I learn, and one idea triggers another. When you give, you receive.

Advocacy

The continued mass killings and individual suicides from coast to coast catch the attention of the American people. However, rather than pointing the finger at the assailants and their families, it is time for all of us to become more involved in public policy that affects the well-being of our nation: public policy that goes beyond gun control and provides greater access to mental health services, recovery, education, research, and support.

Advocacy is our mission. Please help us realize this mission by reading this book, passing it on, and adding to it. What is your story? Where can individuals, with a severe mental illness, find a long-term, comprehensive system, in an open environment? What state? What country? Together we can be the catalyst for change, but we must be relentless in our passion and purpose for improvement. Our mission must be stronger and larger than our personalities or individual differences. As a collective body, having one voice and speaking out together, we can achieve more. Through our voices we provide hope and healing for others. I say, "Continue to let your light shine, it matters. When you let your light shine, you bless someone else. By letting our light shine together, we make a greater impact."

Resiliency

As a family unit we have learned through our experiences and we are graduates from the school of hard knocks. We are in search of truth, social justice, and integrity. Through our journey in life we have witnessed an impairment of ethical values in our society. We know the pain and shame attached to the illness. Ignorance and lack of education about diseases of the brain have had a chilling effect on human relations. According to Albert Einstein, without an ethical culture, there is no salvation for humanity. In this book, we talk about the current system, we uncover barriers to recovery, and we make recommendations regarding what can be done in the future. We want to ignite fire in the belly and get you, the reader, engaged in critical issues and conversations.

Through our truth we offer a human perspective on mental illness. By sharing our personal family story, we are taking a bold step in the hope of contributing to the value of all mankind. Receive our contribution to the field as an inheritance. By studying the past, what worked and what has not worked, what action was taken and what lay dormant, together we can define a better future. All of us together, are better than any one of us alone.

EARLY DETECTION AND INTERVENTION

Why I Love Me So Much

- by Eace Bee

Truth, once you find it, you never want to let it go. I walk through doors I dislike. Schools can no longer harm me because although they dissect me I can't let go of me. I am worth more than the men who tease me through the seasons. The horror of criticism aimed at me hurts, yet you say this is the crew of today's leaders. Their mimics are embarrassing. Maybe we should take a closer look at the definitions of citizenship and leadership. Sometimes I react to dirty remarks and other times I choose not to. I was taught to recognize ignorance so I struggle to retain my character.

Historical Backdrop

This non.-fiction book is for families, teachers, caregivers, and consumers of the system. The case study and memoir is written about my family facing the challenges of a loved one diagnosed with a severe neuro-chemical imbalance. We are acutely aware of the suffering of others and we have the deepest empathy for the ongoing anguish they endure.

It has been my observation that those living with cognitive disorders are often misunderstood and are victims of physical, social and verbal abuse. They are bullied, talked down to, made fun of, and isolated from society. The victims are left with shame, blame, and regret. Almost half of the victims have a dual diagnosis, mental illness plus alcohol or drug abuse. I pose the question, are they trying to escape from what lives inside of them? Or are they trying to escape from a cruel world in which they do not fit in as respected citizens or human beings? Maybe they are trying to escape from both. People with bipolar disorder, major depression, schizophrenia, obsessive-compulsive disorder, eating disorders, anxiety and post-traumatic stress disorder are in our homes, schools, churches, military ranks, hospitals and prisons, on our jobs, and within our communities.

In high school he was preparing for and looking forward to becoming an architect. At the age of sixteen he was struck down and disabled by a crippling mental illness. Eace was hit with the disease at a very vulnerable time in his development. It takes the human brain about twenty years to fully develop. He was diagnosed with severe paranoid schizophrenia, and I believe he is also schizoaffective. In addition to hearing voices and having other psychotic symptoms, he has severe mood swings. He has been living with this condition for twenty years now. He can be in and out of hospitals every three months or every three weeks. Not too long ago, he was able to make it two years before being hospitalized. Thanksgiving and Christmas seem to elevate his stress.

As a lifelong educator and nationally known leader, I was absolutely shattered and lost when mental illness struck my son like a bolt of lightning. During my darkest days, I felt as if I were alone, out at sea, in a sinking ship without a sail or a lifeboat. Schizophrenia affects a number of senses—people with schizophrenia can suffer from visual, auditory, kinesthetic, emotional, and tactile hallucinations. The disease interferes with, functions of the brain including, reasoning skills. It affects one in one hundred people. Symptoms arise from a failure of the chemical processes in the brain to function properly. It is a neurological disease that affects the nervous system. The behavior of an affected person may be awkward, unpredictable, and impulsive. Those diagnosed with this devastating disease are in a nightmare they cannot escape. Motor functions, speech, and even eye movements may be affected. Individuals with schizophrenia may not always make sense to others when they talk, because their words and thoughts can be disorganized and disconnected.

A person with schizophrenia is usually starved for friendship and acceptance. Personality changes hurt the social life of afflicted individuals. Usually, people dealing with a psychotic disease do not like to be touched. Exchanging phone numbers with friends is almost foreign to them. I believe that as a defense mechanism one exhibits lack of remorse for antisocial behaviors. At times I thought I was the only friend my son had (other than his cousins Adrienne and Daniel). He once said to me, "I am a sick, dying man. I just want you to show me a little more kindness. When the sickness erupts, it affects my behavior. I want to trust folks but I don't have the energy, I don't have the fire and gas to be around others. I feel bad about the things that have happened to me. You are a good friend, Mom, and I hope you will be around forever. We are friends. I pray to the Lord that I will get better."

Not Recognizing or Understanding What We Observe

I thought my son's mental illness was the first case I had personally experienced. However, when I looked back over my educational career I remembered those individual students with peculiar behavior who stood out and may have slipped through the cracks. Because I had no training or experience with mental illness at the time, I rationalized unusual student behaviors. For instance, as an elementary principal, at School A, there was a first –grade student we called "the runner." With no notice she would shoot out of the classroom like a speeding bullet, down the hall, and into the streets, running to some unknown destination. I rationalized that this student was afraid of separation and her mother must have deserted her at one time and she was afraid of it happening again. Today I would have the staff and parents explore the possibility of a separation or anxiety disorder as well as panic attacks.

In School B there was a third grade student who would hide under a staircase in the school or under his desk in the classroom. I attributed his behavior to the fact that his father was incarcerated and he had a hard time coping with his absence. In reality, he was dealing with a great deal of emotional trauma and possibly an anxiety disorder or even a post-traumatic stress (PTS) disorder. I noted that his behavior, with the male director, at the after school YMCA program was completely different.

School C presented different challenges. In a school assembly of 750 students, I noticed one student who vividly stood out. According to school standards, this fifth grade student was exhibiting inappropriate behavior. I summoned his mother for a conference just to learn that she was afraid of her own son. She showed bruises on her arms and body as evidence. I was in a pickle, I knew how to report parents to child protective services (CPS) but I did not know what to do when children were abusing their parents. The mother was obviously under a great deal of mental distress and her son may have been suffering from oppositional defiant disorder (ODD).

Medication for Young Children

At School C, I was astonished by the number of students who would line up in the hall each day at lunchtime to take their medication. I thought this daily routine was inappropriate—a total mistreatment and over identification of students with special needs. While I never voiced this opinion aloud (due to the culture of the school and the community), I was certain that giving an enormous amount of elementary students medication was not the answer. But in School C, one sixth-grade student stood out. If he did not have his medication, his behavior—or misbehavior—disrupted the entire school day for him and everyone around him. His episodes caused my first real acceptance that some students cannot function in society without their medication.

Building Relationships

When I was a high school English teacher, a student violently rose up against me one day. I suspected that he was high on drugs. Today, two things come to mind. Number one, as previously mentioned, it is not uncommon for those with mental illness to have a dual diagnosis. Number two, building relationships matter. As a result of the relationships that I had built over time with other students, when the aforementioned individual student stood up to attack me, the rest of the class stood up to protect me. Lesson learned. Don't ever underestimate the power of building relationships and trust.

Special Education

Instead of getting medical treatment in early childhood and adolescence, students are often diverted into special education and/or counseling. Even educators can have the misconception that young people who have a mental illness or those referred to special education lack intelligence. I have witnessed cases where students qualified for special education in one area and were considered gifted in another. However, the current educational system is misguided and rarely deals with such discrepancies. Therefore, these students are usually removed from the gifted and talented list and funneled into special education instead. When I was a principal, most of the training for students with special needs was focused on "crack babies."

During my career in education I was a member of the National Alliance of Black School Educators. One of the primary goals for members of the organization is to reduce the overabundance of black children, particularly black boys, being referred to special education. We don't want to put a label on a child that will follow him throughout his schooling. Once students are identified as needing "special" services, that classification is rarely changed. It is a road to no escape. However, when it comes to mental illness or emotional trauma, research indicates: the longer students wait to get help, the more severe the consequences of the disease. What information can and should we use to open up further inquiry and study?

I now realize that there may be a gap in research related to racial disproportionality and special education. There has been much discussion about how black boys are perceived by their usually white, middle-class, female teachers. However, have we thoroughly explored mental health and wellness related to early psychosis or emotional traumas that some students may have experienced? In other words, are we investigating the depth of the problem and how we can counteract it?

We all act on the knowledge, experiences, and expectations that we bring to a situation, and we can't act on what we don't know. As stated, I have reviewed entrance plans into special services for students. However, I have not personally witnessed an exit or recovery plan. A diagnosis of a mental illness, or learning disability, should not necessarily lead to a life sentence.

Recognize the difference between symptoms of mental illness, a learning disability, and individuals who may have been deprived of basic vicarious experiences. In other words, a person can be dysfunctional if they never learned certain behaviors or gained specific knowledge. Example: a child in third grade (eight years old) has been secluded in his home for years and is coming to school for the first time. He lacks verbal, behavioral, and developmental skills. His parents are on crack. Does the child have a learning and behavioral disability or is he behind because he has never been taught or exposed to an adequate and interactive social environment?

Public Schools' IEP:

Almost everyone has to come through a public classroom. Therefore, one of the best chances for early detection and intervention is through our schools. The goal is to prevent extreme deterioration to the brain. Are there specific signs to look for in young people? What prevention and intervention strategies can be used to help our youth succeed? I have heard kindergarten teachers share that they know when something is off, or can predict what child will be incarcerated later in life. If this is the case, rather than just talking about it, can something be done about it? Build a strong support system. Don't just set learning goals for students but have goals for teachers and families as well.

Identify the Need

Let's consider the facts. Mental illness is the leading cause for hospitalization in children from one to seventeen years of age. One in five children will experience mental confusion. Approximately every one in ten students will experience a serious mental or emotional disorder. Children who are in foster care are two to four times more likely to experience a mental disease. Seventy percent of youth in state and local juvenile systems have a mental illness. Fifty percent of students aged fourteen and older, with mental illness, drop out of school. Suicide is the third leading cause of death among those aged fifteen to twenty-four. More than twenty-five percent of college students have been diagnosed or treated by a professional for a mental condition. We cannot and should not continue to ignore these statistics (www.nami.org/CAAC).

Examine Human Resources

So that teachers have time for the art of pedagogy, allocate nontraditional resources and services to support them. School principals will tell you that traditional counselors have been assigned so many extra duties that they seldom have time to actually provide counseling for students. In order to increase services and meet the needs of students today, encourage schools to collaborate and integrate with other service providers. At the district level, consider staffing resources such as: police officers trained in mental health issues, campus-based therapist(s), a counseling and referral center, licensed social workers, and someone who can conduct psychological evaluations. Offer training and professional development for teachers, staff and parents on suicide prevention and how to recognize symptoms and behaviors related to the early onset of mental illness or mental distress.

<u>Provide</u> Special Services and Opportunities

I am not encouraging over-identification of students to be funneled into special education classes. What I am encouraging is a system of increased support for teachers, students, and families. Rather than automatically lowering educational standards via modifications, examine instructional teaching practices and make accommodations as needed. Provide mental health training and presentations for educators, families and students.

Learning disabilities, behavioral problems, emotional challenges, and speech and language impairment are all separate issues and cannot not be lumped under one label and basically treated the same. Currently students needing special services are identified and categorized by the symptoms and performances they display. *Attention deficit/hyperactivity disorder (ADHD), oppositional defiant disorder (ODD), conduct disorder (CD), mood disorder, depression*, and *anxiety* are some of the categories used. My question is, what are we really doing to address the needs of the identified populations? Research has shown that intensive early intervention can have a profound impact and yield positive results. Yet school funding systems are not reflective of the advances in research. Providing every student with an appropriate education, and leaving no child behind, takes adequate funding, resources, and services. While the need for "special" services is exploding, fiscal responsibility has stagnated. Fully fund special education at 40% higher than the per pupil allocation and allow integrated services for students who need them.

Be innovative at the high school level and utilize programs such as AmeriCorps, vocational education and dual credit opportunities. Through vocational education programs, students can gain work experience and leave high school already certified in a particular area. Through the AmeriCorps program, one can earn credit for high school and work. In addition, after so many hours of work and school combined, they can qualify for a post-secondary scholarship. In the dual credit program students can earn high school and college credit at the same time. To be ready for students with special needs, it should be required that every college provide a mental health center.

Too few people and far too few minorities are working in the mental health field. If we are serious about preparing students for opportunities in this field, in the twenty-first century, a K-16 pipeline and state curriculum must focus on higher levels of science and math, social studies tied to cultural competency, and technology-related classes, courses, and research. School districts and institutions of higher education have the responsibility to utilize strategies to make college more affordable and worth the students' time. Rather than having students incur a lifetime of debt, provide scholarships, residency slots, internships, stipends and grants, particularly for minorities, and particularly for those majoring in psychiatry. In the mental health and wellness field: psychiatrists, psychologists, counselors, social workers and nurses are all a high-priority.

EMOTIONAL STAGES, CONCLUSIONS AND SUGGESTIONS

I Lost My Mind!
-Eace Bee

I lost my mind,
I think it is out there somewhere stranded
For someone to find.
In the meantime, I am out of work and branded.
Please, be kind!
The journey through my journal is where I can be candid.
For writing is my job and I just want to brand it!

Emotional Stages, Conclusions and Suggestions

When dealing with any type of devastating chronic illness, it is normal to go through a range of emotional stages. You can't work through the emotional stages until you acknowledge them. Different stages at different times can include: denial, confusion, fear, grief, frustration, hopelessness, guilt and blame. You don't have to stay stuck in one stage and you don't have to let it define you. As a caregiver, or invested relative, what emotional stages are you experiencing? What emotional stages is the victim experiencing? When someone in the family is suffering with an illness, it definitely affects other family members.

Victim's Story

My name is Eace Bee. I had a good life and was doing well socially with associates, friends, and girlfriends. I was a good student. I began to build my résumé by holding down a few jobs in high school. At one time I wanted to be an architect and later my passion transformed to wanting to be a rapper. Today my passions and hobbies are writing, music, and drawing. I enjoy being artistic and creative and I am learning to roll with the stinging punches that attempt to knock me out. Following are the stages of emotional trauma I went through, and continue to go through, since being diagnosed with a disabling disease.

Denial

I had high hopes and dreams of becoming an architect. I was always smart and placed in gifted and talented classes. I was preparing to become a contributing member of society. However, later in life, around my senior year in high school, things began to change. It was hard for me to focus and my aspirations became clouded. Finally, I was diagnosed with a chemical imbalance which effects brain functioning. I refused to believe it. Nevertheless, my disease became my oppressor and I was imprisoned.

Frustration

I feel like I'm in a bad dream that I can't come out of. Simple tasks have become complex. It is almost like learning how to walk and talk again. Society's guidelines are sometimes unbearable for me. I struggle to fit in so I try to blend into the crowds. Sometimes I resent my mother for treating me like a baby and I resent others for pitying and disrespecting me. Why do others feel as though they have to interfere? Life is suppose to be about opportunity! Right? Where is the justice for me?

My Reality

I hear voices so I talk back to them. Because I hear voices that others cannot hear, I think I may have supernatural powers, but others look at me like I'm strange. I have collective word banks flowing at the same time to an unrecognized rhythm. I can literally feel blood dripping from my arms and into my stomach. Maybe I have a tumor in my brain. Sometimes it feels like there is a possum in my stomach. At other times I hear bees, lizards, and even the fan communicating with me. I try to pretend to the outside world that it does not hurt but on the inside it hurts a lot. When it is hard to get through the day, I want to scream or destroy something to release the negative energy.

Hopelessness

The voices are always present. I have nowhere to go and nowhere to escape to. It is difficult to have a condition such as mine. I catch cruelty every day from the outside world. Yet, I struggle to suppress my rage. It is hard for me to share other people's world and they certainly can't share mine. I understand what they say but they act as if they can't understand what I say. I holler inside and sometimes out loud. I feel lost. I'm afraid that no one understands me so I show strength by rejecting others and the things around me. How did I get here? How can I escape? Instead of going to college as I imagined, I end up in hospitals instead. How did I become a victim of this form of slavery? Group homes, hospitals, and psychiatrists are my new norm.

Reluctant Acceptance

Sometimes I try to take medication, but it is still a real challenge for me. If I don't take medication they take me to the hospital. Where is the justice in that? I get tired of my mom having the police roll up on me.

I used to enjoy going to the movies with my mother and family. However, the last time I accompanied my mom to the movies, when I took a break, I was surrounded by four policemen. They said I looked suspicious. I had on three to four layers of clothes but do I really look that different from everyone else? I don't tell anyone else how to dress. Since then I haven't wanted to go to another movie theater. I would rather watch movies at home where it's safe. As a result, my mom bought me a DVD player.

When I first took medication, it zapped all my strength, but others thought I was just being lazy and noncompliant. Today I am supposed to take medication to improve my mind, but the truth is, when I feel better I don't want to take it anymore. I don't like shots either. I am a man and I want to decide what I will do. Even when I think I don't need medication, I try to trust my mother and others who encourage me to do the right thing. Sometimes I love and appreciate my mother but at other times I don't trust her—she's not perfect either.

Recovery

What is important is that I keep trying. God is not finished with me yet. I may have a disease but I don't think it is the one I was diagnosed with. You can't always listen to and believe what the white man says. After hitting rock bottom again and again, acceptance and making progress should be my focus, but it is not like having a broken leg that will heal. Dealing with my illness takes a great deal of ongoing concentration, will, determination, and effort. I get tired. I gave up life as I once knew it and I have to start a new life. I try to come back from my own private Twilight Zone, the Outer Limits of my world, and my own Planet Z. My travels and episodic trips go beyond what you see on television. I don't have to go to the movies to see a drama or horror flick because they play in my head every day, all day.

I am still trying to learn to stop saying no to those who are in a position to help me and help guide and determine my fate. But it is a continuous struggle because I am a grown man. Looking at pictures is supposed to remind me of my upbringing, friends, and family. However, I admit that I often don't recognize the person that I use to be. My mother tells me that I can reflect on where I was, where I am, and the picture I can paint for my future—through faith, hope, and God's mercy and grace.

I still struggle with distinguishing between what is real and what is not. When I hear voices, I am told that I am hallucinating. The voices and people are real to me and it is difficult to shut the damn things up. That is when my speech doesn't make sense to anyone but me. It feels like someone is trying to take over my body.

One thing that was instilled in me when I was young was to study, and go home and study some more. I think education or a job would help me find my freedom and self-worth. Sometimes I am very discouraged but I don't want to give up. I try to remember that there is a certain voice and tone I should talk to my mother and others in. There is a certain way that I should not look at others because it is intimidating to them and may cause conflict. I try not to be angry or worry excessively about everything, but sometimes I do. Inside I feel that I am gentle and vulnerable but outside, in order to survive, I have to be hostile and no one had better mess with me. Sometimes I just don't give a damn! Writing is a safe way for me to socialize and communicate.

I have a chemical imbalance in my brain that acts as a mind repellent. I want to work but the Office of Rehabilitation didn't help me. Pain is not being able to work. I don't understand, I won't bother anyone, I catch on fast, and I know how to follow instructions. I keep my shame hidden because I don't want others to feel sorry for me. Having a mental illness does not mean that you are incompetent or stupid.

Sometimes I feel like a cold body. If I die or commit suicide you will ask, "Why?" But I feel that you never cared in the first place. I am the only real person in touch with me. Therefore, my intrinsic joy and pride must come from within. Like a branch falling from a tall tree, I have missed out on a lot of good things. Suffering with mental confusion is like losing sunshine from my life. I have to go the extra mile to complete tasks and overcome obstacles. My spirit is broken. The truth is, as I navigate through this world, no one shares my special journey with me, and that is why I love me so much. Though I struggle with agony, stress, and dishonor, it is through self-love that I continue to build my self-confidence. While I keep my soul entrapped with God, maybe men will open their hearts here on earth.

Conclusions and Suggestions – Mother's Voice

Workforce and Educational Opportunities

Access to jobs and educational opportunities are important factors to consider when reviewing or updating jail diversion programs. Over the years Eace has tried, unsuccessfully, to regain his dignity by taking higher education classes and applying for jobs. A person suffering from severe mental illness already has a self-esteem problem; stigma further erodes confidence. As an empowerment strategy, increase vocational training and job opportunities for those with a diagnosed mental illness. Include transportation as a support mechanism. At this time, most residential facilities provide transportation only to the doctor for prescriptions and some only provide shelter.

Implement evidence-based programs that help the most seriously ill. Allow those with mental illness to be productive, have a feeling of self-worth, and give back to the community. This would be a huge step in the right direction. We do this to some degree but we need to do so much more! This progressive step alone would be like a Make-a-Wish Foundation for the chronically mentally ill. Individuals need to feel whole and not hopeless.

The severity of mental illnesses varies widely. Just because someone has a disability does not mean that he or she is not intelligent. Students who can continue their education or hold a job should do so. Representatives of students with disabilities, and the Department of Health and Human Services, should continue outreach to recruit and support diagnosed individuals. In the areas of education, training, and work-force development, there is a need for more funding, grants and scholarships.

A Mother In Anguish

Mother's Story: Emotional Stages Before and After Diagnosis

I had a well-mannered son who was handsome (and still is), a sharp dresser, smart, and driven. He was crawling at five months and walking at nine months old. He was reading by the time he was three years old. Eace was ready for kindergarten. In addition to reading, he knew his colors and numbers. He had good reasoning skills and by second grade he was writing his own books. In the back of a book, called *The Turkey Trot*, there was an Interests or About the Author section and he said he wanted to be a doctor. He liked swimming, skating, competitive games, riding a bike, playing basketball, and working with manipulatives such as Lego's, building blocks, numbers, letters and puzzles. I concluded that he was on the right path.

Eace was in gifted and talented classes in elementary school. I understood the school-to-prison pipeline. Basically, prison projections correlate with third grade reading scores. My child was not at risk. In third grade he was at or above a third grade reading level. In high school, due to one specific role model, Eace aspired to go to college and become an architect. He was excited and responsible when he got his first, and only, car.

We were extremely close and he was exceptionally respectful to me and others. From my perspective there is nothing like the bond and relationship between a mother and her children. Eace had it all, including the girls. I often told him when he was in high school that he could be a model. Joy flowed in abundance and he possessed all the blessings that God had to offer him. That is why I became confused when his behavior and appearance changed drastically when he was around sixteen years old. As a mother I instinctively knew in my heart that something was not quite right, something was going terribly wrong. He was quickly deteriorating. He demanded that I stop calling him Eace. "My name is Maleke!"

Confusion

In middle school my son began to have trouble with his stomach and digestive system. Even then he gave me a hard time about taking his medication. As a junior in high school Eace aced the ACT, SAT, and state exams with no problem. During his senior year in high school, I took him to take a test to be a manager of a store. I noted that it was taking him an exceptionally long time to process the answers. When he didn't pass, I was told that the test-taker had to score at or above a designated grade level. Now I was really confused.

In addition to cognitive, and health and wellness changes, I noticed behavioral changes. Eace began to walk differently, more like a Neanderthal. He began to slack off with his appearance. Small tasks like holding a fork, carrying a plate, and cooking became complex and overwhelming. His behavior became moody, compulsive, aggressive, and excessive. For instance, he would put twenty packets of sugar in a small cup of coffee. He would verbally attack me, my mother, and others who loved him. His moods, rude outbreaks, and low emotional intelligence were all baffling. His judgment and focus became blurred and all of a sudden, rather than an architect, he wanted to be a rapper. I knew that something devastating was transforming my son. What mysterious, foreign, frightening condition could this be?

During the early stages of his illness, I began to take him to doctors. However, the doctors did not discover anything wrong with him. I could not give up. I was desperate. I was a relentless mother in search of answers and solutions. Having worked as a results-driven, high-profile educator at the classroom, school, district and state levels, I was not ready to accept that I could help other people's children but not my own child. Taking the example of a brain-injured person, I decided I could re-teach Eace basic independent living skills. I was confused but I knew that something was definitely wrong. Something had gone through my son's brain and reasoning skills like a forest fire.

Eace was just as confused as I was. As though he needed reassurance, he started asking me if I was really his mother. He must have been hallucinating when he shared with me that the catfish and fries on his plate were warning him that the broccoli was poison and not to eat it.

Blame

As far as I could tell, Eace's behavior and growth was consistent and predictable from infancy to age sixteen. Since the age of two or three, I had raised Eace as a single mother. I saw how his father, David Bee, would continuously promise to pick him up, but he seldom did. Even if his father was trying to get back at me, I could not understand how he could treat his own son so heartlessly. For days and even weeks at a time, Eace refused to get in his bed and insisted on being prepared for his dad if or when he arrived. He would sit on the stairs outside the house. After it got dark he would come and sit on the stairs inside the house. Using his hands to prop up his head, he would sit there for hours at a time. He waited and he waited and he waited, time and time again. What type of man does this to his own son? From this mother's perspective, only a cruel, heartless, and irresponsible one. When Eace hurts I hurt. I too experienced the agony of his father's neglect and mistreatment toward him. I believed that his dad's neglect had a significant effect on my son's emotional state, but this was the painful reality we had to confront. I believe that early abuse and neglect from the ages of zero to three and from three to five years, combined with predetermined biological features, can trigger anxiety, emotional distress, and trauma. My son felt abandoned and he was under serious emotional distress. Are genetics and nurturing intertwined in brain development?

As a mother who also works with families professionally, I have observed firsthand the excruciating pain children experience when they desperately seek the love of an absent father or a father who is not really present in their lives. In elementary school, every time they had Donut's with Dad, Eace came down with a stomach ache and did not want to go to school. Eace's father seldom came around, but when he did, his conversation consisted of a stream of petty criticisms aimed directly at Eace. The result of such neglect and disrespect increases the likelihood that the child affected will become involved in gangs and drugs. It is alarming how many males have never heard their father say, "I love you Son, I am proud of you, I believe in you. You have what it takes to make it." Basically, all children need a solid foundation made of love, stability, nourishment, encouragement, security, direction, and hope. A lingering bitterness haunts boys if they do not have the involvement of a father or responsible male figure in their lives (Pickles, 2012).

As I searched for answers, I continued to blame others. Someone must have done something to my son. Cultural beliefs and norms began to kick in. I considered that my ex-husband and his new wife were both from Louisiana. Even though, for the most part, I kept this thought to myself, I wondered if they had placed some type of voodoo on my son. Maybe they had put something in his food. Yes, I went there. It is not uncommon in some cultures to believe that someone has created a potion to physically and mentally disable someone else, or worked roots or cast hexes. Even today some believe that mentally challenged people are possessed by demons or an evil spirit —and that the only way to get rid of that spirit is to cast it out through exorcism and prayer or through a two headed doctor.

I went from blaming Eace's father to blaming myself. I should have demanded that Eace have more structure and responsibility in his life while growing up. Also, I played a part in separating from his father. My search for answers was like a snowball at the top of a hill, as it rolled down it grew bigger and bigger until it was unstoppable. Being unfamiliar and uneducated in the field of biological chemical imbalances and brain disorders, I was clueless and in denial. I was overcome with anger, fear, grief, and sometimes rage.

Guilt

I wondered what I had missed in Eace's early life and what signs I had failed to see. In early childhood, there were no signs of anything unusual to come. However, he would wander off from the fenced backyard and down the street on his Big Wheel. In elementary school he begin to have terrible nightmares. In addition, he would wait until the last minute to finish his homework assignments. It was difficult to get him to do his chores around the house but to earn extra money he would ask the neighbors to help with their yard or take out their trash. Further, he would beg for the same thing over and over and over again, until he thought he had worn me out. Sometime between elementary school and middle school, he would become exceptionally disturbed when his grandmother would purchase gifts for her other grandsons who may have been viewed as less fortunate. He felt extremely left out and resentful. In middle school (junior high) he stopped participating in activities that he was passionate about, like basketball. But are these behaviors so unnatural that they would stand out from those of any other young child or adolescent?

I wondered if the forceps that the doctor used to pull him out during delivery had caused damage, after all, I could clearly see the marks of trauma on his forehead. It was not uncommon in the 1970's for mothers to reshape the top and front of their babies head. There must be a scientific reason why this practice did not continue into the twenty-first century. Some research points to lack of vitamin B3 (niacin) or sodium as a factor in the development of schizophrenia. Another study indicates that a chemical found in cat litter might contribute. When I heard about the cat litter I immediately thought about how my older brother had insisted on my children having a cat.

I wondered and speculated all of the time. As a single mom, I felt guilty and I worried like Martha in the Bible. I had to work to provide for my children and I was not always accessible to them. I felt as though I had let my son and daughter down by not providing them with a father. To compensate, I stayed involved in community activities and I made certain that my children were exposed to positive and responsible male role models. I realized that I could be a good mother but that it was hard to substitute for a good father. In my excessive and vicious search to make sense of the situation, my thoughts quickly reverted back to Eace's father.

During Eace's junior year in high school, I was presented with an opportunity for advancement in my career, but it meant relocating. Eace had two to three months left of his junior year. Rather than disrupt his schooling, I saw this as an opportunity for him to finally bond with his father. His father embraced the idea and immediately filed for child support. During this time I would make the three-hundred-mile trip every weekend to see my son. One weekend I was horrified when I discovered that my son was homeless: he had been kicked out of his father's house and into the streets. No one had informed me about the ousting. I quickly rented a van and literally kidnapped my own son to take him back to live with me. I carried with me the burden of guilt. Why did I ever leave my son with his father? The debonair young man that I had left only a few months earlier was now broken and disoriented, someone I could barely recognize. He could have been mistaken for a vagrant, or a runaway. Yet, I was still clinging to the vision of what my son could become.

Fear

Having my son close to me once again was comforting but it was also frightening. I moved from confusion and blame to fear. My son's bedroom was on the second floor, right down the hall from mine. I heard conversations but I knew no one had come up the stairs. Anyone entering the second floor would have to pass by my bedroom first. I also decided that Eace could not, in the middle of the night, sneak others through his bedroom window. We lived in a tall two-story home. Nevertheless, the voices continued—intense, violent, vicious, and argumentative. To think of the possibility of having gang members, vagrants or squatters in my home was unconscionable.

I clearly remember the night I gathered up the courage to prove that Eace was not sneaking others into his room. I opened the door not knowing what I would really face. All the voices existed in his head, in his unique world of senses that was difficult for others to understand. He was sitting in the corner on the floor. I sat on the floor with him and I held him my arms and told him how much I loved him. To him the voices in his head were real. Not knowing whom to call, I was finally assured that the Department of Mental Health, and the Health and Human Services Commission, would see him the next morning. I just had to make it through the night. My body was curled up in a ball and my bedroom door was locked. I prayed for our survival. His behavior terrified me. I had never seen anything like it. The next morning, as I drove Eace to his appointment, he spoke irrationally about people in other cars. He felt uncomfortable and stated that the people in the passing cars next to us were staring at him, conspiring against him, and talking about him.

As we talked to the representative at the Department of Mental Health, someone gave the OK to call the police and have Eace transported to the hospital. Seeing my son handcuffed, for the first time, and carried away for his irrational behavior and thoughts shocked me. One of the greatest devastations for a mother is to witness her son handcuffed, pleading to his mom for help, and then hauled away by the police. Taking charge and doing the right thing for my son, results in the kind of heartbreak that a mother never gets use to.

It was from Eace's initial involuntary visit to the hospital that we first heard the diagnosis *paranoid schizophrenia*. Neither one of us truly knew what it meant, but I believe we were both petrified. "Where do we go from here? Is there anywhere to go? How do we get there?" He was in the hospital for about two weeks. On our way home, we passed the homeless on the streets, and for the first time, from behind the windshield, I saw them in a different light. That could have been my son out there. There was very little separating the homeless on the street from my own son. Eace related to them well—too well. I knew we had a long journey ahead of us.

In spite of his diagnosis, both Eace and I were determined to get his high school diploma. He was never suspended or expelled from school. His last six months, of high school, was spent at an alternative school which allowed him to graduate with his classmates.

Hopelessness

A sense of hopelessness swept over Eace and me alike. The next twenty years were a roller coaster ride via hell. His refusing to take his medication remains the biggest hurdle. Who wants to give in to such a dark diagnosis? After all, I am certain that he still doesn't fully understand what hit him so hard that it disarmed and disabled him. Can you imagine waking up one day and not knowing who you are? We tried medication after medication, doctor after doctor. Sometimes I wondered if he could take it anymore, sometimes I wondered if I could take it anymore. We were on waiting lists to see doctors and on waiting lists to receive housing. If we missed an appointment or raised questions at a doctor's office, it was not unusual for the doctor to dismiss us without giving us an opportunity to reschedule.

My professional positions elevated my family profile. Nevertheless, I still managed to break the glass ceiling and all of the stereotypical profiles. As a black, single mother, I was now a CEO with a special needs child. When God shows you favor, there is nothing that man, here on earth, can do about it. Regardless of my professional responsibilities, I was determined not to leave my son with his father again. As a result of travel, I was able to experience and compare the lack of services allocated to mental health and wellness, in different parts of the country. I moved Eace with me from the Southwest to the Midwest, from the Midwest to the West coast and back to the Southwest. On the west coast he had his own efficiency but was evicted because he was accused of harassing a young lady and she reported him. He moved into a group home. It was difficult to get him to leave the west coast. I actually had to leave him behind for a few months. However, with the help of others, when I finally convinced him to join me, I sent him a bus ticket with explicit instructions. Before he could make it to his destination, a media blitz went out. Some lady reported that she had found my run-away son. Eace was never a run away. His appearance and behavior makes others nervous and suspicious. They point, they stare, they gossip, and they say he looks threatening. He is an easy target for discrimination. Eace needs, and has needed for some years now, adequate treatment. Shake your head at the system, not at my son.

Witnessing the way that others stigmatized, abused, and made fun of my son was heartbreaking. His self-esteem, his dreams for the future, were shattered. On the other hand, the way my son treated those who loved him (such as family members) was unacceptable and emotionally wrenching to witness. He could suddenly turn these intimidating looks on loved ones and strangers alike, as though they were the enemy. In the meantime, gaining access to information and piecing together programs was, and still is, a nightmare. The only time I saw my own mother break down and cry was when my son was being handcuffed and begging his grandma to help him. These experiences wrench the heart.

Besides finding a psychiatrist to provide medication, finding decent housing can also be a horrifying experience. When funds are cut and people with special needs are dumped into the streets, there is a significant increase in the prison population. Because of the shortage of housing, finding residencies where caregivers are knowledgeable about cultural competency is challenging.

Hopelessness leads to depression, and alcohol and drugs are often used to mask fear and pain. When my son hit absolute rock bottom, as his mother, so did I. Eace was institutionalized and doctors and staff from the forensic unit made grim predictions about his future and his possibility for recovery. As a mother I was devastated. I was dying from a broken heart.

In my lifetime, as a black woman, I have experienced both blatant and covert racism. However, my experiences are nothing compared to how my black son with a cognitive disability is treated. I am afraid that one day Eace may feel too hopeless and miserable. He once said, "What good am I? I have nothing to offer others but pain. I might as well be dead, others would be better off." When I hear statements like this from my son, I grieve. I share with him that tomorrow is a brand new day. I tell him to pray and to have faith. I tell him not to give up hope. I reiterate that he has to trust God more. I never forget to tell him that I love him. As a result of the stress from grieving, I make concrete plans that reflect faith and hope. Faith without work is dead.

The Acceptance Process:

Living with a chronic mental illness is difficult for the diagnosed person and his family. Part of going through the emotional stages is finally accepting that the illness is not necessarily any one person's fault. Accept the hand that is dealt to you and learn how to play it. I know, easier said than done. I began to read a lot of literature and research studies on schizophrenia, mood disorders, and cognitive coaching.

One day, while I was sitting in church, the pastor casually announced that the National Alliance on Mental Illness (NAMI) would be making a presentation at Monday night's Bible study. I remember sitting in the balcony thinking to myself, "Did I hear the announcement correctly?" I had heard of NAMI and had even been a contributing member. As far as I could tell, the organization hadn't really helped me. But I was not going to take a chance on missing the meeting. I showed up that Monday evening.

"Oh my God! My precious Lord, you promised that you would not put any more on us than we can bear." The individuals who gave the Sharing Hope presentation used language that I could relate to, they understood what I was going through. I finally had someone to talk to. Putting a face to NAMI was much different from just reading a newsletter. Before the presentation I would not have dared say the words *schizophrenia* or *mental illness*, especially not in the black community. Doing so would invite criticism, stereotypes, taunting, disconnect and more grief. For the most part, even my relatives were not much help. I would constantly hear, "Damn, I am glad I am not you."

I took the presentation at the church a step further. I began to take training classes. I met affected people and family members who understood me. They became my new family. For the first time in a long time, I was in a safe environment where everyone understood what I was going through. As I listened to the personal stories from those around the table, I had a flashback to mothers killing their newborn babies during slavery. I had a better understanding of why they would rather kill their little miracles as opposed to letting them suffer the tragedies and horror of slavery.

During the break in one of the training workshops, participants called to check on their loved ones. "Did you take your medication?" We created our own "normal" environment. After one break I can remember coming in very excited because I had just used one of the communication strategies I'd learned in a conversation with my son, and it worked! I was making progress in connecting with him, and I began to hope again. I became a NAMI *Family-to-Family Education Program* teacher and I also took the *Parents and Teachers as Allies* training and Facilitator training. I understand that when you learn you teach, and when you teach you learn. And it was then that I accepted that I would rather live with my son in his world than live without him in mine.

Through an assimilation exercise I understood the various voices in Eace's head that were competing for his attention and why it would take him so long to respond to a question. Previously, I thought he had a hearing problem. When I took him to the doctor and the results indicated that his hearing was fine, I had assumed he was just ignoring me. I also learned that although a prominent illness may be diagnosed, the patient suffering from schizophrenia may also be suffering from a cluster of symptoms of other illnesses like bipolar, depression, anxiety, and obsessive-compulsive disorder.

There is nothing like an education to give you a different perspective, a better understanding, and critical thinking skills. Rather than trying to come up with solutions on my own, through support groups I learned from others who had already dealt with similar problems and challenges. One of the greatest compliments I received came during a Christmas vacation when Eace decided he was not going to take his medication. I calmly said, "I understand why you don't want to take your medication, and that is your choice. However, this is my home and I need you to pack your things so I can take you back to your home now." My daughter smiled and said, "Mom, I can tell you have been through training! Wow!" I did not cause the illness nor can I cure it, but I can love my son just as he is and support him through recovery.

Moving from acceptance to recovery was not an easy transition for me. I wanted to explore and research every possibility available for my son. I began to go deeper into metacognition and how one thinks, and how our beliefs affect our behavior.

During the acceptance phase of the illness, my results driven behavior kicked in. I retired at the age of fifty-five and was able to do consulting work. What man meant for evil, God meant for good. This freed me up to do other things that were personally of importance to me. As previously stated, as a determined mother on a mission to save her child, I began to make a case study of Eace's condition. I learned everything I could to try to make sense of his illness. After twenty years of going through the cycle of emotions, I was stuck between acceptance and the recovery phase.

At one point, I even embraced the thought of being his sole caregiver. After exhausting all of my options and after learning as much as I could about Eace's illness, I decided that I would take charge. I thought I had become quite the expert. We made it together for seven months. Keeping track of and explaining accumulated expenses is a job within itself. One skill that Eace never lost was the ability to track money. Without a calculator or paper and pencil, he can add, subtract, multiply and divide. He can precisely tell you, down to the penny what is due. I made a mistake once and he pointed it out just by glancing at the paper.

Eace takes praise well but not criticism. Rather than pointing the finger, I tried to remember, in the heat of the moments, to just talk about how I felt. I also had to learn that I could not win every battle and sometimes I needed to let him win. Helping me with chores and outside work seem to give Eace a sense of worth. If he could, I know that he would want to take care of me and he has voiced this desire on several occasions. His heart is in the right place, it is the illness that gets in the way.

When Eace lived with me, it was hard for me to sleep at night. In addition to slamming the cabinets shut, I never knew if something was on fire on the stove or in the microwave. He refused to take his medication and I was tired of begging him to do so. With his food preparation and cooking, dripping coffee all over the house and other unsanitary rituals, I could not live that way any longer.

I became exhausted, burnt out and depleted. I was so appalled by his living conditions that I thought I might be having a mental melt down. I ran away from my own home, with only the clothes on my back, and checked into a hotel. Have you ever been so frustrated and disgusted that you felt like walking off and leaving everything behind? That is when I think of stories like Helen Keller and how she made it in spite of the odds.

My son is under considerable situational stress and his eyes sometimes swell with tears. When his eyes are filled with tears, so are mine. When my son left the house, I was left, once again, with constant uncertainty and worry. I seek a least restrictive environment that can address his real needs.

The Complex Brain

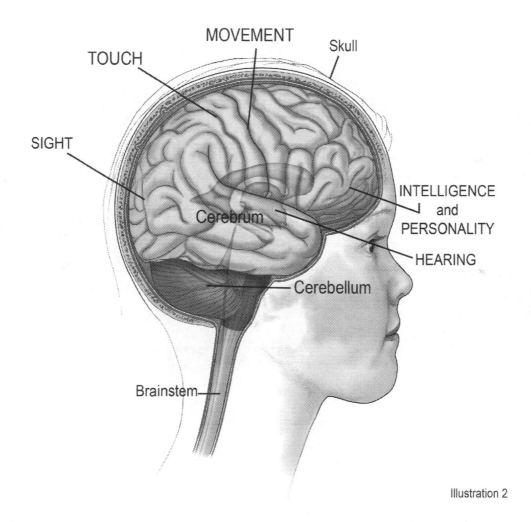

Illustration 2

The Complex Brain and Chronic Mental Illness

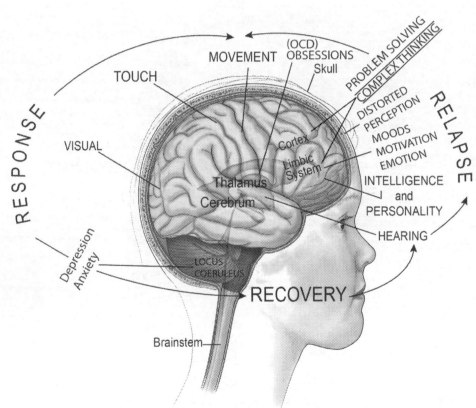

Hypothesis: When you think better, you speak better.

The brain is a complex and vital three-pound organ. It has one hundred billion nerve cells with hundreds of trillions of connections among them. It uses more than one hundred different chemicals, including serotonin and dopamine. There are right and left brain hemispheres. The localization theory of brain functioning acknowledges that the hemispheres of the brain have a working relationship with each other, but also that specific functions exist in distinct areas. The brain controls body movements, thoughts, feelings, and memories. There is the thinking or intellectual part of the brain, the emotional part, and the survival component. Knowing more about the living brain gives me a different perspective on the cliché "You are getting on my last nerve."

Treatment - Measuring Progress, Performance and Improvement

As with any chronic disease, a relapse or setback is always a possibility. The goal, however, is to stabilize the individual to prevent further deterioration of the brain. The effectiveness of the medicine depends on whether it is used regularly and if there are consistent levels in the blood. When there is no medication in the system or the medication is no longer effective, the patient relapses. For my son, depletion can occur very quickly. Recovery is a journey where someone makes a conscious effort, every day, to take care of himself. There is no one single model for recovery and recovery may look different for each consumer. It depends on the individual's baseline. Signs of relapse and response to medications may also be very different for various patients. I read a *Family-to-Family* lesson that stated, "After a psychotic break of any kind, the usual period of recuperation can take as long as two years." One goal is to keep from having a relapse or at least to keep the relapses as far apart as possible.

The good news is that mental illness, for the majority of the population, is treatable. Schizophrenia tends to be more severe than other forms of mental illness, but it is treatable, and you can become aware of the acute and distinct symptoms of an individual doing better or worse, moving forward or backward. "Peace, progress, protection, and healing" are words that have entered my daily prayer. Doctors used to ask me questions that I could not answer. That was before I began documenting my observations and actually taking the time to listen to and talk with Eace.

Relapse Mode
I am in a war zone and I AM AFRAID!

Eace Bee

Illustration 3

I have learned that Eace may have short bouts or episodes of symptoms that do not necessarily lead to a full-blown relapse. On average the psychotic bouts, bizarre behaviors, or hallucinations can last anywhere from five to thirty minutes. I have also learned that if I can remain calm he will usually settle down. However, if he is in the wrong environment or is around another aggressor, as illustration number 3 demonstrates, things can go terribly wrong. This is why crisis intervention training for first responders is so critical. Remember, individuals suffering from the disease of mental illness are far more likely to be victims of violence than perpetrators.

The family's goal for Eace is for him to have appropriate and effective medication, communication, support from others, and to live in a safe environment where comprehensive services and intervention is provided. Healthy codependence is what we want for him. However, Eace wants a place that he can call his own. He wants independence. As you can see, there is a gap between what the family wants and what the consumer wants. This is one example of a real issue that must continuously be grappled with. However, we all agree that in spite of his disabling disease, to the greatest extent possible, he deserves to keep his dignity and integrity. He deserves an improved quality of life.

Recovery entails time to recuperate and time to rebuild. For example, every time my mother went in for chemotherapy, she needed time to recover and rebuild her strength. Unfortunately, every time she began to recover from the chemo, it was time to go back for another treatment. The cycle of any serious illness can be devastating and draining.

I have personally found it quite frustrating that every time Eace sees a new doctor, or goes to the hospital or a new facility, his medication and dosage are changed. While I am open to new research and science, I do not want my son used as a guinea pig and if I do not keep up with what he is taking, when he is taking it, and what is working and what is not, it will leave us with no baseline to discus, nothing to debate or go to bat for.

There is no cure for most mental illnesses, so plan to plan—and then to re-plan. It is an ongoing process. I find that doing practical things relieves stress and worry. Reaching recovery is a journey and requires a continuous learning model and making adjustments along the way. What signs does your loved one show when slipping back into relapse mode? What are signs that they are on the road to recovery? You need a resource tool that will help you evaluate the effectiveness of treatment.

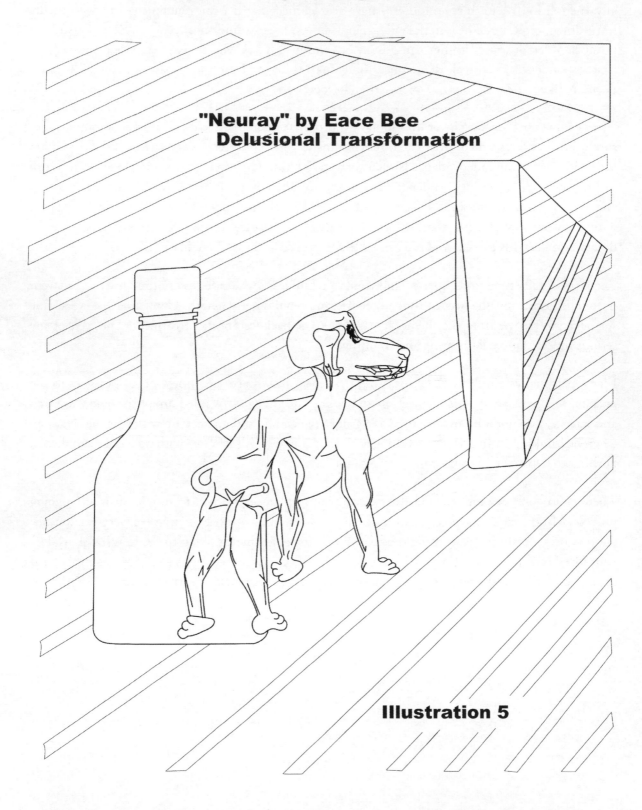

"Neuray" by Eace Bee
Delusional Transformation

Illustration 5

How many of you can relate to some of the random behaviors listed below? Make your own list. It will come in handy when you are talking with your loved one's doctor or when your loved one is hospitalized. The more information you have regarding behaviors, the less paralyzed you will become during a crisis that can freeze you in a state of fear, pain, and grief.

What do relapse and recovery look like? A random sample has been provided below.

Relapse	**Recovery**
Refuses to take his medication	Names medication he takes
Hears angry, violent voices	May hear voices but smiles
Aggressive, agitated, irritable	Calm, sense of humor
Sleepless nights, pacing	Sleeps at night
Suspicious, resentful	Cordial
Petty crimes	No solicitation or panhandling
Dangerous to himself or others	Nonthreatening
Deterioration of grooming	Improved personal grooming
Disoriented, depressed	Present, recognizes others
Vulgar and belligerent	Respectful, manages emotions
Use of alcohol or drugs	Sobriety
Feels worthless	Has goals and ideas
Wears up to three layers of clothing	Dresses appropriately for the season
Tight jaws/fists, raging eyes	Relaxed muscles, calmer eyes
Carries large fifteen-pound bag (full of papers that only he can interpret)	Is able to leave the bag behind
Wears red bandanna	Absence of red bandanna

Define and Address the Problem

A problem is never solved without a solution. I search for ways to enhance wellness and to keep Eace from regressing back into his illness. When he refuses to take medication, I push for injections. I have learned that once a prescription becomes generic, the research on the drug stops. Where are we with neuroscience and what role is it currently playing among the mentally ill?

I plan to put forth an effort to locate Eace's original MRI, taken years ago, so that it may be compared to a current one. I have learned that the ability to problem-solve and brainstorm keeps me from getting overwhelmed, stuck in the here and now, and frozen in fear and hopelessness.

Like it or not, the consumer must take some responsibility. As caregivers there are certain problems that cannot be resolved. A consumer, for instance, refusing to take medication, pills or injectable(s), is usually doomed and there is nothing you can do about it on a long term basis. Emergency hospitalizations become a Band-Aid and temporary fix. Another example of a problem you can't fix is, if the consumer insists on using alcohol or drugs. They can go to rehabilitation programs but again it is a temporary fix. Unless the consumer has decided that he wants to quit, he will go right back to the same addiction pattern once he is released.

My Recovery

Truth is the will not to allow ourselves to be deceived or distracted from reality by blaming others or ourselves. I am certain that you have heard that you don't forgive for the sake of the other person, you do it for yourself. When you forgive, it can't change the past, but it can change your future. It took me many years to let go of judging others and myself for Eace's state of mind. I took a detour to the road of recovery. I remind myself every day that I'm not the judge, God is. Whom do you need to forgive to set yourself free? What do you need to further investigate or examine in order to let go?

As a mother, I finally realized that it was not only my son who had to recover. Little by little, I had been committing my own suicide. I even had a near-death experience. I had completely depleted myself. Eace said, "Mom, why are you always worrying about me? When are you going to start taking care of yourself?"

In order to reclaim my own life I had to feel as though I was worthy. I had to free myself from the cycle of fear, blame, guilt, confusion, and anger and I had to re-grip hope, faith and resilience. I had to learn all I could about my son's emotional and biological illness. Then I had to find resources to meet Eace's needs and fill in the gaps. What I found was very little resources and nearly nothing to fill the gaps of need. My son was in and out of private hospitals every month or every other month. The only reason this was possible was because of the secondary private insurance I carry on him. Bottom line, my son needs long term care in a facility that offers comprehensive continuity of services. However, no such facility is available. Therefore, where is the recovery?

Recovery for me as a mother is to respect my son as the remarkable and good man that he is. He has an illness but I refuse to define him by his illness. Whether it is cancer, heart disease, high blood pressure, alcoholism, diabetes, or AIDS, an illness is an illness. As we go on with our lives, we try to keep it under control the best we can.

Part of the recovery process for me is advocacy. Reaching out and touching the lives of other individuals and families dealing with mental illness is rewarding. My reward is in the karma of helping others. I am always blessed by someone else who shares his or her story with me. I knew that the efforts were all worth it when my son said to me, "Mom, I love you, and you just don't know how good it feels to have someone to talk to." I dare you to make a difference in someone's life!

Self-Care

Some things you do have control over. Resiliency is not automatic. It comes from protecting and taking care of yourself. I know what it is like to be totally depleted through stress. Give yourself permission to get on with your life. I will continue to spend quality time with myself, and others as feasible. I will say no without guilt to some of the activities, duties, and engagements that could consume my time and energy. I will make keeping a balance among my spiritual, physical, and mental health a priority. Spas, pedicures, hair salons, swimming and strolls through the park will be part of my routines. Finally, I am going to continue to plan short trips and getaways. I deserve these things and more. I am important, and in order to give to someone else I must first be kind to myself. I am learning to be my own best friend.

If you have assumed the role of caretaker, you can easily become overwhelmed, both emotionally and physically. Know your limits. To the greatest extent possible, surround yourself with positive people, people who will lift you up and make you smile. The foundation for a strong relationship is based on mutual trust and respect. Intentionally select friends and associates who will say good things about you behind your back as well as to your face. All people are important and some individuals teach you what not to say or do. As for stress, be aware that you are already in a vulnerable position and that negativity weakens your immune system. Be with those who bring out the best in you, not the stress in you. In a two-minute interview, what positive things can you say about yourself? It is not the load that breaks you down, it is how you carry it. Are you living or are you merely existing? As we mature and define who we are, we shed the belief that we have to please everyone else to be OK.

Conclusions and Suggestions – Mother's Voice

Housing

To increase options for affordable housing, there is a need for more assistance dollars. It is a mother's living nightmare to envision her child homeless, on the streets without protection, food, or shelter. Housing and shelter for the disabled is difficult to find and usually abysmal; yet we know that housing is a critical component of the recovery and rehabilitation process. For individuals needing more support, or individuals with capped income, limited housing is available. Living facilities that will guarantee daily meals, a room with someone else or others, and monitoring of medication is as good as it gets. Certain group homes are located to protect the well-being of the residents and others are not.

Available housing differs according to the severity of the illness. Choices may include nursing homes, group homes, boarding homes, shelters, private facilities, family care homes, halfway houses, efficiencies, apartments, county homes, and state hospitals. Housing options are often temporary. I am not certain what the solution is but cities may want to consider moving the homeless, who are mentally ill, into interim care facilities and off the streets. This could increase opportunities for comprehensive care and decrease the recidivism rate. The current system of arresting the homeless for trespassing, destroying the few belongings they have, and then releasing them back onto the streets with nowhere to go is not working. It is a vicious cycle. It appears that we have more respect and compassion for animals than we do for human beings. We put forth an effort to provide stray or abused animals with food and shelter while working to find a stable home for them. Let's put more effort into rescuing human-beings.

Fifteen percent of adult male prisoners and thirty-one percent of adult female prisoners have serious mental illness. The largest mental health facility in Texas is the Harris County Jail. Similar trends are: Rikers Island, Cook County Jail, and the Los Angeles Jail. With a felony record, housing becomes even more dismal.

Require caregivers to take training in dealing with the mentally challenged population. Not everyone has the patience for such demanding and draining work. For instance, at one of the last group homes my son stayed in, he was hit in the back of the head with a hammer by one of the employees. Many turn their head to such incidents and unlicensed facilities because, in reality, there is no place else for them to go.

I remember receiving a phone call one day that new efficiencies were being built and they would be ready in a few months. I jumped at the opportunity and immediately went downtown to pick up an application. After convincing my son to sign the papers, I dropped the information in the mail in a timely manner. I received a phone call informing me that a $15.00 money order was needed in order to process the application. The same day I put the money order in the mail box. A few weeks later I received another phone call telling me that I needed an application to go with the $15.00 money order. They stated that they did not accept applications via the mail. Bottom line, they had lost the application and all of the efficiencies were now filled. It is this type of lack of follow through that can cause one to reach their boiling point. Maybe it is due to a shortage in staffing and human resources, but lack of responsibility and accountability is all too common in the mental health field.

To secure housing with adequate services requires that you sign up on a waiting list. For some housing programs, it can take up to ten years for a consumer's name to come up. Request that the legislature provide more funding and noncompetitive grants for private and public housing programs. Privately run programs of good quality must be available for those at all levels of the economic stratum.

Coordinate and Integrate Services

There is a need for an ongoing, long-term, seamless accountability system that addresses prevention, treatment, and rehabilitation services. At the state level, there is disconnect and lack of communication among institutions. The right hand does not know what the left hand is doing. Care received in jails, prisons, homeless services and hospitals are not connected to the community and community services are not connected to one another. Twenty-five percent of all homeless people are mentally ill and many more have addiction disorders.

Be prepared to make a list of needed support services and then find out where the services may be offered: disability income, housing options and assistance with food, case management, medical doctor, dentist, service provider as payee, psychotherapy, medication, peer-to-peer support, work force development, and appointing an executor of your Will, to name a few. Someone dependable is needed to bring all the pieces together and close the gaps in services. That someone is usually a family member, case manager, or a paid entity.

Due to a dysfunctional system, it is not unusual for victims of mental illness to develop a sense of interdependence among themselves. In one city, for instance, it took six months just to get Eace into the system. Eace was hospitalized six times in six months. Upon being released from the hospital he was to report to a facility that provided him with a temporary prescription. Before he could get an appointment with a doctor at another facility, he had already relapsed. After six months, we finally got him in the city's mental health system. I was so excited! We finally made it to first base, or at least that is what I thought.

An appointment was made to go to another facility across town to meet with a team that would help monitor Eace's health and well-being. We were so anxious that we showed up a week early. The next week that we returned, we were an hour early. We checked in at the front desk and waited to find out what support services were available to us. An hour and fifteen minutes went by. That is when the receptionist informed us that the case manager said that he did not have an appointment with us. Needless to say, my blood pressure shot up along with my temperament. Once again, hospitalization was the only option for getting Eace stabilized and getting him the help he deserved. On this night in particular, I can remember waking up the next morning grateful that I had not had a stroke or an aneurysm.

The next day I spoke with the case manager. He informed me that he makes his own appointments, not the office. The misinformation and lack of communication, within the system, and at the same facility, is totally unacceptable, intolerable, and a living nightmare.

There are gaps in the system and a lack of human resources. An integrated health care system, like a one-stop shop is needed. Confront the most basic needs of consumers head on. Call for a system that addresses physical, dental, visual, mental and substance abuse needs. A system that provides housing as well as job opportunities. Address the whole person as a viable human-being. This means taking a closer look at how resources are being allocated and distributed.

Insurance Benefits and the Parity Law

Insurance for behavioral or mental disorders has primarily been focused on seventy-two hour crisis stabilization and minimum length of stay, making long-term and comprehensive treatment less likely. Through the Affordable Health Care Act and the Mental Health Parity Law, mental health has been brought back into the mainstream of the debate on health and wellness. I know it takes time to, make changes to our current structure and to, change mind sets. It won't be done overnight but for the betterment of our society and our country, it will be well worth the effort to do it as soon as possible.

Improve quality of care for those with a chronic illness. The Mental Health Parity Act, enacted in 2008, under the Affordable Care Act, calls for equity under the law. Without charging more for co-payments, without charging more for co-payments, reimburse mental health providers for services at the same rate as other medical-health-care providers. In other words, remove treatment limits and treat mental illness like any other chronic physical disease—remember, the brain is an organ and part of the body. I have personally experienced doctors wanting to keep my son in the hospital for longer periods but being unable to because the primary decision makers were insurance providers. Shift more power to the psychiatrists and practitioners – those actually in the field.

Make it transparent what the federal government will reimburse to state and private hospitals. It is my understanding that private hospitals have reduced their psychiatric beds because Medicare and Medicaid typically pay less for inpatient mental health care than for medical care. Yet, Medicaid remains the largest provider of mental health services in the country.

Eace is released prematurely from hospitals. Individuals such as Eace are dumped back into society, ready or not, with no long term after care treatment or recovery plan in place. Early discharges lead to repeated hospitalizations and brain deterioration. I can only imagine what his life could look like if he received full treatment. The cost of rehabilitation may be included under insurance plans and designated providers are eligible to deliver post-care and interim services.

More support is needed for affordable health care and the parity law. Fear of capping out or running out of lifetime mental health benefits should not be an issue. Strengthen Medicaid and Medicare to ensure affordable high-quality care. Advocate that more is spent on mental health and that recovery is more than a pipe dream, it is a priority. Break the cycle of transitional trips to jail where victims lose benefits resulting in no insurance and no income.

Increase the Number of Hospital Beds

Increase hospital days, beds, and services. Strengthen, expand, and even re-engineer our current mental health policy. Allow Medicaid reimbursement for persons with mental illness who need care in a state psychiatric hospital. Across America, the deinstitutionalization movement has had an incomprehensible impact on medical services.

From 1841 to 1854, mental health advocate Dorothea Dix initiated major efforts to move the mentally ill to state hospitals and facilities that would support their recovery. In the twenty-first century, we are in the same predicament and fighting the same battle. State and private hospital beds, for mental health, have decreased and are still declining.

As a result of lack of access to services, there are more people with psychiatric illnesses living on America's streets, or incarcerated, than receiving medical care: this is unconscionable and inhumane! Jails have become holding places until beds are available. Overall, thirty-five thousand hospital beds are available in our country for the mentally ill. However, 356,000 of the mentally ill are located in our jails and prisons. That is a tenfold difference in terms of where our most vulnerable population is located. Blacks and other minorities are more likely to be incarcerated and often receive a poorer quality of mental health care.

Sibling's Story

My name is Honey Bee and I am an educator by profession. I taught secondary science for seventeen years and I am currently an administrator in the field of education. My approach to education is holistic. I believe in understanding the development of a child, where he or she is, and where he or she comes from in terms of background, culture, and ethnicity. These factors cannot and should not be underestimated. I believe all these indicators are important when it comes to growth and education. In addition, I consider birth order and other factors important, such as whether a child comes from a single-parent home or one where multiple families are living together. As opposed to just passing a class, my goal for each and every student is that the student in question see the big picture and the value of getting an education. As a result, I believe in creating an environment that will encourage and motivate students to want more for themselves and learn the importance of giving back to the community.

In spite of my education and training, I found myself experiencing many different emotions when it came to my younger brother who was diagnosed with schizophrenia. Below I describe my experiences and emotions during this challenging journey.

Fear

When I first learned of Eace's diagnosis, I didn't know how to react. I wanted to be helpful, but I didn't know what to say or do. As his older sister, I was lost. I was always afraid that he would hurt himself, my mother, or my children. I was afraid that he would never get better and I was afraid that I would never be able to enjoy being with my brother again. I missed his company. We could no longer bond like normal siblings. My greatest fear, even today, is that my brother will pass away before I can make a positive impact in his life because I just don't know what to do to help him.

Grief

Every time my brother goes through the cycle of not taking his medication, my heart hurts, and it affects the entire family. He can be very territorial of mom. When disciplining my children he also interferes. You can tell when there is no medication in his system, and it doesn't take long to disappear. During this time my brother is volatile and feels that the entire world is against him. This is when my mother has to call the police and the Emergency Medical Services to have him taken away. Every time my mother has to go through this process, as a mother, I feel her grief. I grieve over the fact that Eace has not been fully present. I wanted nieces and nephews. I wanted a sister-in-law to hang out with and cousins for my children to grow up and bond with. I have had to accept that this dream is now unrealistic.

Guilt

I feel guilty when I do not take the time to visit my brother often enough. I really feel guilty when he is in the hospital and I am not able to help. Because of my lack of understanding of his illness, and other emotions, it is difficult for me to be of greater assistance. When Eace first became ill, our relationship changed. I became more distant. Making meaningful connections is difficult.

Shame

When people from his past ask me about Eace, I don't know what to say. I don't know how to explain his condition and I don't believe that others know enough to understand his situation. Further, as a result of his illness, I'm ashamed and afraid of his being labeled as "crazy." I always used to say that he was doing well even when he wasn't. While I feel guilt and shame about not being more forthcoming, I also feel the need to protect my brother. Everyone doesn't need to know our business, nor can everyone handle our business, nor can we handle everyone knowing our business. My mother shared with me a response she heard from one of her support group members. When people ask about Eace, I can simply reply, "He is still trying to find himself."

Acceptance

When I was able to accept that my brother had a legitimate illness, I began to better understand the symptoms associated with the illness. This allowed me to better connect with him and recognize his symptoms as part of the illness. As a result, talking about him to others became easier. Because my brother has been diagnosed as paranoid schizophrenic, when I talk with him I accept that I won't always understand his thought process or what he is trying to say. Jumping from one subject to another and saying things that I do not understand is not uncommon for a person suffering from his condition. Previously, the lack of effective communication between the two of us would really frustrate and irritate me. Although I still want to communicate with him, I accept that sometimes I won't understand what he is saying. It is difficult to pretend that we are having a normal conversation when in reality we are not.

I once asked someone in the mental health field how I could improve conversations with my brother. She suggested that I take in every three to four words and try to block the others out. She further explained that my brother is obviously listening to different voices at the same time. In other words, although it sometimes sounds as if he is talking nonsense, if you listen closely, there is some truth and relevance embedded in his babbling. To make things easier for myself, I now listen to his conversations in a different way.

Also, I now have a totally different perspective of my brother being hospitalized. His admittance use to sadden and devastate me. Now, when I hear that he has been hospitalized, I am glad to hear that he is getting the help that he needs.

Knowledge is power. Advocating for the rights of the mentally ill has become my mother's passion. My passion is consistent: I desire to help young people realize their potential. In order for one to realize their potential, they have to know who they are and have a vision of who they want to become.

True ID: The Word Salad
by Eace Bee

* *, church and street preceding, seasonal inhibitions, one look at the wind ready to enjoy the feeling of game and play toys. A brochure as the spot of redemption a scorching makes a fidelity undertaking now a foul, pushing buttons a * to back up poured in importable self. Apply when the obstacle was a set improbable a curtain may have to fall. Thunders it storms where I plotted in the sky is that automatic running into number red and black 5 art full of fluid and does it notches the artifact skull no portion still a brain of *. The going of a momentum exists and leagues round together in the moment we all perish to survive daily. When I get a perishable moment, I need pork * then to bail against trauma. There's an optimistic sunken dish labeling for me, taking care of myself spiritually and having fair play.

*Denotes words not found in the dictionary: Wakca, Adhesits, studecy, ponnedy, iatric

Conclusions and Suggestions - Mother's Voice

Community Crisis Intervention

To avoid jail and emergency hospitalization, cities and counties are encouraged to construct a true twenty-four-hour crisis hotline center and mobile crisis services that work. To cut hospitalization and incarceration costs, increase treatment within communities. What would this look and feel like? Bottom line, increase access to treatment, when we need it and where we need it. When mileage is not even considered as a factor, restricted access to treatment is discriminatory against the mentally ill.

I remember calling a crisis hotline center and even though it was right down the street, I was told that I was not in the right county and I was given another phone number to call. With no questions asked, I dialed the other number. The person who answered the phone asked me to call 911. On another day, I called a crisis intervention team hotline. It was between three and five a.m. I was informed that although there was always someone available to answer the phone, no one would be available in the office to assist me until ten in the morning. As crisis occurs, like a mobile library that may come to your community, insist on a mobile crisis outreach center ready to assist in stabilizing individuals affected by mental illness. Making an appointment to come out at a later time or date is not addressing the immediate crisis or unique situation.

Access to immediate assessment and stabilization services is needed. If someone needs to go to the hospital, a crisis team can make the experience less traumatic and restraint would be limited during transport. Twenty-four-hour psychiatric centers, that are truly available, and adequately staffed, is strongly encouraged. I remember taking Eace to a crisis center and filling out paper work just to be told that there was no one available to see him at the time and that we had to come back on another day. It would have been nice if he had at least been referred to a crisis stabilization unit or a facility where he could have been under extended observation. As opposed to limited city-wide services, I suggest that governors take a closer Look at statewide models that work. Professional development and training for staff will help to ensure adequate implementation of the model.

One of my greatest fears, as a mother, is that my son will be shot, choked, or tased to death during an emergency call for help. Please understand that Eace is sick, he is not a criminal. While training for first responders and caretakers is in place, more needs to be done. When dialing 911 I always ask for a mental health officer. While this approach has been successful for me, a lack of hospital beds often leaves no place to take the patient. In the interim, I pray that suicide is not a path my son chooses and that jail or prison does not become his new hospital.

HIPPA Law

Parents who provide care out of love, and caregivers who have the responsibility to provide quality service, should have access to treatment plans, prescriptions and doctor appointments. I understand that this is a controversial issue, but seriously consider making it illegal for someone with a biological brain disorder and impaired thinking to remain sick and refuse medical treatment. While HIPPA (the Health Insurance Portability and Accountability Act) is intended to protect the patient, today it may stand in the way of treatment for those who desperately need it. This is when supported decision making is needed.

Many, if not most, are not aware that they are severely ill (a neurological condition called *Anosognosia*). Currently, the only way these victims can get help is by posing a danger to themselves or others. If it were your loved one, would you rather see him incarcerated, in the hospital, or supported by a comprehensive mental health team? Even if doctors refuse to meet with me and talk to me about my son's condition, I still communicate with them in writing.

On the other hand, Eace loves the sense of power that the HIPPA law gives him. During one hospitalization he informed the health-care providers that they could only communicate with me if the word did not start with an X or end with a Z. Also, a K could not be in the middle of a word. This became our legal working document. To be safe, the nurse and social worker wrote everything out that they said to me. This is time consuming. I want to re-iterate that while the HIPPA law provides medical privacy rights for the patient, nothing prohibits a caretaker or family member from providing the doctor with information or talking about symptoms that may be of concern.

DIVERSITY AND CULTURAL COMPETENCE

Vision

It is our vision that mental health will become the cornerstone for public health. Stigma will be eradicated. Through economic stimulus, there will be increased affordable and supportive housing opportunities. Everyone will have access to comprehensive, high quality services and culturally competent health care.

Diversity and Cultural Competence

Disparities and Barriers to Treatment

When we talk about breaking down barriers to access quality mental health care, it should be understood that some barriers are universal and cross color and economic lines. Consumers may desire a sense of normalcy, and they do not want to be sick and have to take pills for the rest of their lives. They do not want to be stigmatized and they may not actually realize that they are sick, a condition called anosognosia. This is an example of a barrier that crosses lines of color and socioeconomic status. However, I find it interesting that, while consumers of the system may not be able to recognize when they are ill, they can recognize the illness in someone else.

Nevertheless, specific barriers affect particular cultures disproportionately. As a result, minority, racial, and indigent subgroups and communities usually receive fragmented and lower quality services. Cultural disparities are often cited among Asians/Pacific Islanders, Hispanics, and blacks. Members of these and other cultures may face language and communication barriers as well as lack of cultural competency on the part of providers. Poor people have always been and remain vulnerable. As we continue to move toward a more global and diverse society, regardless of our differences, everyone deserves high quality health care.

Systemic Barriers

The tale of two cities is Eaces personal experience in two very different economic areas and cultures. Compare the contrast and delivery of services between the two systems.

The Tale of Two Cities

City A	City B
The system is pro-active.	The system is re-active.
Streamline intake process. Can be done over the phone in fifteen minutes.	All intake done in person, takes an hour and a half.
Appointments are set up like any other doctor appointment.	Appointments are set up but it does not matter. First come, first served.
One stop shop for medication, counseling and support.	Multiple locations for medication and other support services.
Effective communication within the system.	Poor communication within the system and lack of execution of services.

In City A, once Eace had to be hospitalized, the case manager, I will call Bob, made us feel very uncomfortable. He started following my son and me around the facility as if we were thieves or thugs. In addition, he immediately stopped making home visits. It was as though he was trying to chase us across the tracks, to City B, to get services. Entering a cold, uncaring and disrespectful culture and climate, where one is not respected, will make consumers not want to return. Initially, while services across the track were viewed to be of poorer quality, I quickly found that some locations were much better than others.

Fear and Lack of Trust

From color barriers to chains of prejudice, slavery continues to have an impact on our society today. Blacks are 50 percent less likely to seek treatment than whites. When they do seek it, blacks often receive poorer quality of care because of fear on the part of the consumer and the provider. The provider may have fallen prey to the images presented in newspapers and on television, viewing minorities as assertive criminals, agitated gangsters and worthless drug addicts. On the other hand there is often a low trust level on the part of the consumer because people of color may not see anyone in the mental health field, the justice system, or emergency services who look like them. Yet, these are the people who have the authority to lock them up. As a result, the white man, or even the Asian man, may be viewed as the enemy or the oppressor.

Communication Strategies

Today's generation communicate by texting, e-mailing, Instagram, websites, blogging and word of mouth. While brochures and written material are still of value, it is important to acknowledge modern communication styles as well. In addition, having providers who can speak the consumer's first language adds value. Also, blacks are more comfortable talking about physical ailments rather than mental delusions. For instance, rather than saying he is hallucinating, he may say he has a headache.

Historical Racial Injustice

The history and the legacy of racial injustice in America is well documented and ethical clinical studies have not necessarily been a part of the black experience. For instance, the Tuskegee syphilis experiment, conducted from 1932 to 1972 by the US government, has not been forgotten. The Tuskegee study was closed only because of a whistleblower and although the penicillin treatment for syphilis was available in the 1940s, the lives of 399 black men were destroyed. This number does not include their wives or children.

In the case of Henrietta Lacks, her cells were removed without her knowledge, for experimental purposes, at Johns Hopkins University. Henrietta, a black woman, died in 1951 at the age of thirty-one. However, her cells were cloned and sold. The HeLa cells have been used in medical research since the 1950s. In 2010, Dr. Roland Pattillo, of Morehouse College, donated a headstone for Lacks's unmarked grave.

How can African-Americans really be certain that their blood samples and genetic materials are not being removed and used for unauthorized research today? (Placebo studies are still being conducted, but on a smaller scale and with the permission of the consumer.)

Spiritual and Cultural Beliefs

Medical needs may be blurred by one's spiritual and cultural beliefs. For instance, the belief that the disease is caused by demons, roots, or a hex. Rather than seeking medical advice, an affected person may seek spiritual advice, advice from a two-headed doctor, or embrace what he or she believes to be a predetermined fate. On the other hand, however, both prayer and the belief that there is a God fuels hope and faith.

Lack of Transportation

Not understanding how to navigate the complex process, to gaining access to services, may cause many to drop out of the system by default. Further, lack of transportation impairs many consumers and families from taking advantage of services and opportunities that may be available to them. Fragmented services offered in different parts of town can be cumbersome for some and impossible for others.

Inadequate Health Insurance

Medicaid is the largest provider of mental health, yet it reimburses at a lower rate causing less hospital beds and reduced services. In addition, the fact that Medicaid has not been accepted by all states, leaves too many people unnecessarily uninsured. Until the Parity Law is actually enforced, individuals with mental illness still face the obstacle of limited days of service and hospitalization. This lessens the possibility for recovery, hope and healing. The revolving door from homelessness, incarceration, and even hospitalization may also negatively impact insurance benefits.

Stigma

Our society has a legacy of stigmatizing and ostracizing those who have an abnormal brain. Yet, an abnormal heart or an abnormal kidney is more acceptable. Collectively, we have been cruel and have created an insensitive and hostile environment. In the black community there is a nasty stigma attached to seeing a psychiatrist. Therefore, there is lack of knowledge about mental health and wellness. Stigma, stereotypes, lack of knowledge, and the shame of mental illness lead to suffering in silence and keeping the issue in the closet. Further, individuals do not want the stigma to stand in the way of finding, obtaining, and maintaining employment.

What does stigma look like in the black community? Disrespect—loud, tasteless, and cruel jokes in front of your face and behind your back. Stories about the victim and the victim's family that devalue their worth. Gossip and derogatory comments. Everyone talking at once or chiming in. The misfortune of the victim is used for entertainment by some and bullying by others. Physical, sexual, and emotional abuse are common. Victims may have no support and no one to talk to. Isolation from friends and family is the norm. Joining a gang to have a connection is not uncommon—after all, the mentally ill often have the qualifications: irritable, angry, aggressive, and a need to belong. In public schools they may be identified as qualifying for special education classes and labeled as having ADHD or behavioral or learning disabilities. They fall victim to the high school dropout rate. The head of household is usually a mother or grandmother.

Outreach to Minority Communities

Don't always expect others to come to you. Reach out and go to them in their neighborhood. Carry a message of what is needed to address mental health issues among minorities. Talk about facts that directly impact them and possible solutions. What is needed is an accessible record of what is working and where. Replicate and fund model programs and research practices that work. Use positive verbal strategies to connect with others and have empathy for what someone else may be going through. Communicate, communicate, and communicate through public awareness and outreach campaigns. Provide outreach and strategically educate and share information within minority communities via programs such as NAMI's *Family-to-Family*, *Parents and Teachers as Allies*, and Sharing Hope.

Inclusive Research

With more research, new treatments are possible. By utilizing genetics, technology and nuero-science, there is hope for the future. However, more inclusive research is needed on the brains of blacks and other minorities. Make stronger connections with brain banks and research centers and find ways to restore faith in our federal government and Ivy League institution(s) of higher education. Instill hope in minority communities by providing the necessary resources for recovery. With economic stimulus comes hope, and with hope comes cooperation. Create the vision of what our mental health system could look like.

Culturally Competent Care

What does culturally competent care look and feel like? Based on the disparities and barriers to treatment cited, a culture reflecting competency is defined as follows:

There is a culture of respect, compassion, and empathy. The consumer has a safe place to tell his or her story. There is a streamline intake application process. Extended outreach and support services are available, including assisted living resources and case managers. Because there is the belief that treatment works, support is provided and hope is encouraged. In addition to scientific knowledge, providers demonstrate emotional intelligence. The strengths and interests of the consumer are underscored and praise and reinforcement are provided as feasible. Cognitive coaching, coping skills and survival strategies are shared. First responders have training in mental illness and know how to approach a crisis situation without stereotyping, profiling, or escalating the situation or circumstances.

Summary: Treatment Works

"The best interest of the patient is the only interest to be considered."
—William J. Mayo, MD

There are a number of inferences that can be drawn from the information and stories shared. Comprehensive treatment works but you have to be able to access services. The work of trailblazers and stigma stompers like Dorothea Dix (1802-1887) and BeBe Moore Campbell (1950-2006), who came before us, should not be forgotten. It has been a long struggle and we are losing ground. Now is the time to pick up the baton for progress and justice. Lack of services for the mentally ill, who have a neurological and chemical imbalance, is a national crisis and the time for change is now!

Disability rights are civil rights. Increased access to services and equal protection under the law is needed. Potential solutions have been discussed and proposed. What is working and what still needs to be improved? The struggle for a better quality of life for the mentally challenged and the disabled is empowered when we lend our voices for the cause of truth, justice, and integrity.

It is difficult to believe that the mentally ill have intentionally been left behind. It is even more difficult to believe that this oversight is due to lack of courage or the will to challenge a dysfunctional system. The current status quo is unacceptable. Unite because there is strength in numbers. Organize because a concrete plan is needed moving forward. Our personal passion will lead us into our purpose. There are promising possibilities for the future.

Support groups are important because they remind us that we are not alone. By sharing personal stories, in a safe environment, we learn from one another. Safe groups can also help us relate to our transformed loved one. Our reward is when we are able to bless someone else while we are going through our own storm.

After hitting rock bottom again, and after suffering from a severe illness for twenty years, on Friday, July 18, 2014, Eace said, "I am sick of being sick, and I am sick and tired of being sick and tired." I replied, "Don't ever give up hope. Always seek rehabilitation, recovery and healing. Face disappointment head on but hold steadfast to faith."

I came to realize that there were three things that I could do immediately to improve the chances of getting increased care for Eace. First, communicate, communicate and communicate. Second, build positive relationships with doctors and providers. Third, set boundaries.

Also, there are three things that the consumer can do to improve his condition. First, admit that he has a disease and he is sick. Second, he has to decide that he is going to be accountable for his well-being by taking prescribed medication. Third, set realistic goals that will bring him joy, a sense of accomplishment and improve his quality of life.

Sometimes are better than others and sometimes things will get better. For instance, I never thought I would live to see the day when Eace would actually call the police for help. He recognized when he was losing control and not feeling well. This was a huge step for Eace. Even the smallest signs of improvement and progress can give us hope.

I remember going to church one Sunday and, on behalf of my son, asking God for a "big" miracle. As I reflect, I not only asked the Lord verbally through prayer, but by writing this book, I am more specific in asking for his favor and grace. Ironically, by the time we got to the summary section of the book, Eace had received long-term care and treatment and he is doing very well. In addition, while seeking adequate housing opportunities that support his recovery, he was assigned to a short-term-transitional program, with an open environment, that provides adequate monitoring, support and resources. The other day I went to visit him and he said, "Mom, I want you to meet my *friend*." Treatment does work – if you can get it. I also believe prayer changes things. There can be a silver lining at the end of your story.

To those who did not personally know Eace nor me, but extended random acts of kindness to ensure that he made it home safely or that he had food and shelter, I thank you more than mere words can express. For those mental health workers who took a special interest in my son, I thank you. For the police officers trained in mental health, thank you for helping us to problem solve. To the doctors, psychiatrists, nurses and social worker(s) who supported his recovery, thank you. In spite of a terribly broken system, you give us hope.

From my perspective and my core truth, I believe that there is a spiritual aspect in caring for those who are sick. Every human being has value and a soul. I believe that God will bestow his mercy and his grace upon those whose minds have been altered and impaired. The more we give to others here on earth, the more God gives to us. Some of us refer to this as karma. As long as you have breath in your body, keep reaching for hope and let everything that has breath praise the Lord. I visualize my son in heaven. He will be whole again and there will be no sickness and there will be no pain—only joy, wellness and peace. Oh, what a day! Eace has fought and is still fighting a good fight.

References

Amador, Xavier Francisco. *I Am Not Sick, I Don't Need Help!: How to Help Someone with Mental Illness Accept Treatment.* 2nd ed. Peconic, NY: Vida Press, 2007.

Burland, Joyce. *NAMI Family-to-Family: A NAMI Peer Education Program for Family Members of Adults Living with Mental Illness* (teacher manual) . 2013.

Fleischhacker, W. Wolfgang, Celso Arango, Paul Arteel, Thomas R. E. Barnes, William Carpenter, Ken Duckworth, Silvana Galderisi, et al. "Schizophrenia—Time to Commit to Policy Change." *Schizophr Bull* 2014 40: S165–S194.

Gionfriddo, Paul. *Losing Tim. How Our Health & Education Systems Failed My Son With Schizophrenia.* Columbia University Press, 2014.

Lovato, Demi. *Staying Strong, 365 days a year.* R.R. Donnelley & Sons Company, 2013.

National Alliance on Mental Illness, Advocate, (pp. 6–10, 14–15), Winter 2014.

Pickles, Patricia. *Are You In A Pickle? Lessons Learned Along The Way; Students' Performance and Achievement Gaps.* Bloomington, IN: AuthorHouse, 2012.

"Loretta Pleasant," Biography.com, http://www.biography.com/people/henrietta-lacks-2136671 (accessed Sep 23, 2014).

Appendix

Philosophy of Education

I believe education is the most important factor in the evolution of an individual and our economy. While it is an educational leader's responsibility to contribute to a work environment that values and supports faculty, staff, and community, there is a reason we put students first. If it were not for the students, educators would not be in great demand or of vital service. The mission is to prepare students for the competitive twenty-first century and our diverse society. Educators must identify students' weaknesses but also build on the strengths and experiences that they bring with them into the classroom. Students can learn and be successful if they are provided with the following: respect, a supportive environment, a well-planned curriculum and syllabus, resources, coaching and direction. The steps and principles of my philosophy are illustrated below.

Establish a Culture of Learning

First, allow students to see themselves in the learning process. It is difficult for students to learn from professors they don't like or respect. Set the tone by creating norms of participation and respect. Also, encourage innovation, critical thinking, and problem-solving skills, debate and questioning techniques. Encourage students to challenge the process. **Second**, in order to produce results, clearly indicate desired outcomes. Instructors begin with purpose and with the end in mind. What do we want students to know and be able to do? The curriculum is thoughtfully aligned with today's society, advanced education, and meaningful employment opportunities. The curriculum also relates to the students' culture and interests. Share goals for performance that are specific, measurable, attainable, results-oriented, and time-sensitive. **Third,** it is essential to align written, taught, and assessed curricula—this allows for ongoing analysis and critical adjustments for improvement. In order to encourage depth of knowledge, provide students with multiple opportunities to demonstrate their understanding of the subject matter. Use students' performance results for reflection(s) and to suggest minor changes and tweaks to the curriculum, teaching, and the learning process. In addition to paper-and-pencil tests, use evidence-based assessments that also include authentic projects. Make individual and group assignments a part of the overall assessment process.

To provide a diverse student body with an exemplary education and a spirit of excellence, one needs a sound pedagogy, a way of teaching—a well-thought-out plan that stretches students to grow—and engaged learning opportunities that are relevant to real-world expectations and skills. My philosophy of education is simple, and transparent, but it is also results-driven. I believe in turning theory into practice and vision into reality.

Patricia L. Pickles, Ph.D.

Philosophy of Education for Those Living with Mental Illness

I believe that treatment, recovery, and stability are the most important factors in the evolution of an individual and our society. It is the responsibility of educators, parents, providers, and caregivers to contribute to a respectful and supportive environment for those diagnosed with mental illnesses. This population is often under-served, disrespected, and misunderstood. There is a great need for better education, more work-force opportunities, and improved services. The mission is to improve the lives of millions of Americans affected by mental illnesses. One of the greatest misconceptions is that these people are stupid and incapable of learning. Nothing could be further from the truth. With proper treatment and accommodations, it is not uncommon for students to qualify for gifted education. These students can continue to flourish and be successful if they are provided with the following: respect, a comprehensive plan of support, adequate resources, coaching, and direction from someone they trust. The steps and principles of my philosophy for people with mental illnesses are listed below.

First, Pursue a Diagnosis Based on Precise Symptoms and Behaviors

It is difficult to work on a plan for recovery if the problem or illness has not been clearly identified. As with cancer, the earlier the illness is identified the better. Every time there is a psychotic episode, there is a chance of more damage to the brain.

Second, Based on the Diagnosis, Seek a Comprehensive Treatment Plan

Medication, counseling, and group support are all significant mechanisms for rebuilding the lost person. A life without attainable goals, plans, and purpose is a life deferred. Also, everyone yearns for the basic needs of love, a sense of belonging, and a sense of contributing to society. We all want meaning in our life and our work. Individual therapy or family counseling is targeted to help a single individual or a single family structure. However, eventually one must interpret the world and determine truth for himself. Support groups allow the consumer to understand that he is not alone in his struggle. There are others in the community who are also facing the same challenges and experiences.

Medication is used to stabilize the chemical imbalance in the brain. It is important to communicate physical and mental effects from medication. This allows for ongoing forensic analysis and for critical adjustments to the medication used for improvement and stabilization.

Third, Identify and Build on the Strengths of the Individual

While minimizing weaknesses, utilize and underscore strengths to maximize growth, recovery, and quality of life. Cultivate experiences that inspire growth.

Fourth, Make Recovery, Stabilization, and Self-Sufficiency the Goals

Recovery may look different for different people, and it depends on their individual performance baseline. In other words, where was the individual and where is he now? Measurement of success should be specific, authentic, and evidence-based. Consumers receiving mental health services are apt to stay in recovery mode longer if they are supported by their families and by comprehensive services. Recovery and self-care may revolve around hygiene for one person and being able to hold a job for another. For someone else it could entail interacting with others or even knowing when to independently check into the hospital. For others it could mean making better choices by weighing the consequences or using restraint to avoid behaviors that might result in discipline, eviction, or arrest.

Education is the most important factor in the evolution of both the individual and society. It addresses the physical, emotional, cognitive, and social aspects of the learner. A spirit of excellence for the mentally ill entails educational opportunities that prepare them for real-work expectations. It is only through education that the stigma of mental illness can be broken. My philosophy of educating the "special needs" population is to be transparent and results-driven.

"Plants are shaped by cultivation and men by education."
—Jean Jacques Rousseau

Patricia L. Pickles, Ph.D.

Language for the Twenty-First Century: Power Talk

We can begin to change the world, one person at a time, by being cognizant of the words we use and how we communicate with and describe others. It is my belief that individuals suffering from mental illness have dignity and worth too. My language should reflect my belief system. I recognize and understand that my voice may not be the only one in my son's head. Therefore, I am determined to be the most positive voice he hears. I don't want my son to feel like a victim, I want him to know that he is a victor who is overcoming tremendous obstacles. Language is the framework for how we think and act and how we make others feel. Language is also a powerful weapon for persuasion.

Language and tone of voice matter. They can make us laugh or make us cry, they can build our self-esteem or tear us down. Think about it: although we know it is not real, we even find ourselves reacting to the language in movies. No one likes to be labeled or associated with a negative word. Use language to cultivate a person's strengths and not his weaknesses.

Below are examples of "old language." What new terms can we consider using in the here and now? This "power talk" strategy can be a relevant lesson in cultural sensitivity and competency, respect, and emotional intelligence.

Language for the 21st Century

Old Language	Power Talk
At-risk students	Students' in at-risk situations
Behavior plan	Success plan
Crazy	Neurological and chemical imbalance
Diversity	Inclusion
Empathy (emotion)	Respect (action)
Idiot	Developmentally delayed
Insanity	Abnormal brain structure
Insane asylum	Psychiatric hospital
Insurmountable obstacles	Manageable challenges
Lunatic	Biological imbalance
Mad	Hallucinating
Shame	Pain
Special education students	Students' with special needs

Ten Strategies to Avoid Relapse: One Mother's Perspective

1) Set boundaries and present options.

2) Avoid ongoing negative criticism. Patience is a virtue.

3) Keep your voice at a low, even tone. Don't fight, and no screaming matches.

4) Use behavior modification. Every chance you get, praise and reinforce positive behavior.

5) Find a peer-to-peer support group. Normalize your loved one's life as much as possible.

6) Seek additional sources of support, such as counseling, psychotherapy, and cognitive coaching.

7) Identify and build on your loved one's strengths and the activities he or she enjoys.

8) Focus: together, set short- and long-term goals, and take small action steps.

9) Strive to establish a good relationship and good rapport.

10) Exemplify hope, courage and faith.

Faith without work is dead. Once I have done all I can do, I know it is time to ask for additional help and support from my savior and Lord Jesus Christ. Sometimes that means letting go and letting God. What ever you believe in, your patience and faith will likely be tested.

Envisioning a Model Mental Health Program

Take time to investigate what is working, where, and why. This is America and I believe we have the fortitude for a more civil approach to how we deal with those suffering from mental illness. Because there is a great need, for adequate affordable housing, in the field of mental health and wellness, I have often thought about opening my own facility and dream of what it would look like. Below is a brief description of my dream for affordable housing.

The overall mission of the independent living facility will be to deliver more effective and comprehensive care. The social and emotional environment that one is in matters. Therefore, I will provide an environment that is stimulating and language-rich. The model will be holistic and will nurture the mind, spirit, and body. It will include a proven integrated model based on strategies that work. The residence or facility would be aesthetically pleasing and peaceful. The program will be responsive to the needs of the consumers. All employees will be required to take training and professional development in understanding and communicating with those with mental illness. Employees will include teachers, a psychiatrist, counselor, security guard, custodian, nurse, nutritionist, social worker, grant writer and driver. The facility will be licensed and monitored by the state.

Mind

To avoid further deterioration of the brain, monitoring of medication management will be provided. There will be integrated counseling, psychotherapy, and behavioral therapy. The ratio of consumers to staffed personel will be a serious consideration. Classes will be provided in art, creative writing, and job-readiness skills. An internal and external work program will be available. Transportation will be provided, as needed, for doctor appointments, work-force development and for those pursuing further education opportunities. Further, consumers will have a quiet library room that they can go to. In addition to books and magazines, there will be computers with software that promotes cognitive thinking.

Spirit and Soul

Bible study classes will be available to support the emotional and spiritual aspects of one's life. Social activities will also be an aspect of the program. Social skills and life skills training will be provided in a relevant environment where practice may be applied in real life situations. To further reinforce individual pride, consumers' creative writing and art work will be displayed.

Positive interactions and socialization is pertinent. A game room will be available with cards, dominoes, checkers, chess, badminton, a pool table or ping pong table and music. In addition, to the game room, opportunities to socialize and to interact will others include peer-to-peer classes and vicarious field trips. Also, families will be encouraged to play a significant role in the consumers' recovery. Training in effective communication strategies and opportunities such as Family-to-Family classes will be offered

Body

Taking care of the body will also be a priority. Diet can significantly affect behavior, mood and other performance measures. Therefore, meals will be planned by a nutritionist. To reduce stress and promote good health, physical exercise and sports activities will be available. If necessary, transportation will be provided. Physicals and other health care needs will be included in services provided. For instance, as in some schools, annual on-site physicals will take place. Dental and vision screenings will also be performed. Family members will be informed of results as feasible.

The environment is a respectful one with healthy boundaries. Consumers will be made aware of a twenty-four-hour crisis hotline they can call for help. The staff will maintain a good working relationship with local first responders like police and community crisis intervention centers.

Inspire New Ways of seeing the Mental-Health-Care System

As you can see from the ideas shared above, a great deal of the facility's success will depend on strong partnerships and integration of services. The staff will be trained to provide individual plans that reflect a person-centered approach to care. We will look for consumers' untapped potential and create an environment that supports innovative opportunities.

We know what works. Although integrated housing, like the framework provided above, may be available, it does not come without challenges. For instance, the waiting list can be more than ten years and most families can't afford the cost of private facilities. The average cost of a private facility is $6,000 a month. Further, the expansion of Medicaid is not supported in all states. Without an environment that supports recovery, long-term treatment is difficult. When we examine what we are paying in hospital costs and incarceration, there is much more that we can do as communities, a society, and as a country. I may be dreaming but life without a dream is deferred.

In conclusion, I have seen a glimmer of hope in a program for jail and hospital diversion. The program is exceptional. The problem is that it is temporary, lasting only up to twenty-one days for those with a dual diagnosis. Long-term continuity of care and comprehensive services in an open setting, for the chronically mentally ill, is desperately needed. When consumers are released from hospitals or jails, it is critical that they be placed in an environment that will support their recovery. Today, although the need is great, a residence like the one described here is almost impossible to find. Being in the wrong environment will only exasperate the condition and the problems associated with mental illness.

About the Editor and Authors - Ending the Silence

Eace Bee is unique and he is smart. He has personality, a sense of humor, and he has a big heart. Do not define or judge Eace by his illness.

www.DrPatriciaPicklesBooks.com

Dr. Patricia L. Pickles is the editor of ***Chronic Mental Illness: A Living Nightmare*** and the author of ***Are You In A Pickle? Lessons Learned Along The Way: Students' Performance And Achievement Gaps***. She will only write or speak about topics that she personally feels passionate about. Dr. Pat is a leader who advocates for individuals with special needs and some of society's most vulnerable sectors. Pickles is on the board of NAMI Austin, a member of Alpha Kappa Alpha Sorority (AKA), and a member of Mount Sinai Missionary Baptist Church.

Eace Bee has never been married and has no children. He is a compassionate, kind and caring human-being. Eace is a high school graduate. He had aspired to be an architect before he was struck down by a thought disorder at the age of sixteen. On several occasions, he attempted to further his education and training. He has held jobs in food service, maintenance, product assembly and creative writing. Eace enjoys reading and writing, drawing and painting, listening to music, swimming and walking. Eace is a member of the National Alliance on Mental Illness (NAMI).

Honey Bee has been married for twenty years and has four children. She is results driven and to get results she focuses on building relationships. Mrs. Bee is a lifelong educator and administrator. She has taught secondary science: biology, chemistry and physics. She is currently an administrator at the secondary level and is working on her Doctor Degree. Honey received her Bachelor's from Jarvis Christian College and her Master's from Prairie View University. Honey enjoys going to theaters, dancing, painting, drawing, Zumba and walking. She is a member of AKA and the Texas Association of Secondary School Principals (TASSP).

Priscilla Bee is a divorced mother with two children. She provides essential and persistent family support, protection and guidance. She is a lifelong educator and administrator. Priscilla taught secondary English literature and reading. She also served as chief administrator overseeing PreK-12 education systems. She has become active in social reform, and provides training opportunities through NAMI Austin. Examples include, *Family-to-Family* and *Parents and Teachers as Ally's*. By rendering support to others through signature research programs, she touches lives, one person at a time. She believes there is healing in hope. Priscilla enjoys swimming, walking, reading, writing, meditating, reflecting and praying. She also enjoys the opportunity to spend quality time with, her children and grandchildren and, positive friends and associates. Priscilla is a member of NAMI.

Printed in the United States
By Bookmasters